OECD ECONOMIC SURVEYS

UNITED STATES

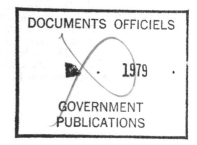

DOCUMENTS OFFICIELS

1979

GOVERNMENT
PUBLICATIONS

ORGANISATION FOR ECONOMIC CO-OPERATION AND DEVELOPMENT

The Organisation for Economic Co-operation and Development (OECD) was set up under a Convention signed in Paris on 14th December, 1960, which provides that the OECD shall promote policies designed:

- to achieve the highest sustainable economic growth and employment and a rising standard of living in Member countries, while maintaining financial stability, and thus to contribute to the development of the world economy;
- to contribute to sound economic expansion in Member as well as non-member countries in the process of economic development;
- to contribute to the expansion of world trade on a multi-lateral, non-discriminatory basis in accordance with international obligations.

The Members of OECD are Australia, Austria, Belgium, Canada, Denmark, Finland, France, the Federal Republic of Germany, Greece, Iceland, Ireland, Italy, Japan, Luxembourg, the Netherlands, New Zealand, Norway, Portugal, Spain, Sweden, Switzerland, Turkey, the United Kingdom and the United States.

The Socialist Federal Republic of Yugoslavia is associated in certain work of the OECD, particularly that of the Economic and Development Review Committee.

***

The annual review of the United States by the OECD Economic and Development Review Committee took place on 16th June, 1977.
The present survey has been updated subsequently.

CONTENTS

INTRODUCTION

When the U.S. economy was reviewed a year ago, a continuation of the recovery with gradually decelerating growth rates was generally expected for 1976 and the first half of 1977. In the event, the erratic quarter-to-quarter growth pattern, which had marked the early upswing phase, continued with the advance in total demand and output falling somewhat short of the Secretariat's predictions. The second half of 1976 was characterised by a marked "pause" in the recovery process, giving rise to concern about the sustainability of the upswing. Towards the end of the year, however, the economy showed renewed strength and despite very unfavourable weather conditions, the first quarter of this year saw output advancing at an annual rate of almost 7 per cent. Prospects for a sustained recovery up to the middle of next year, with further reductions in unemployment, seem favourable. The short-term inflation outlook, though, is less comforting: the underlying rate of inflation seems stuck in the 6 per cent range, with temporary factors worsening recent price performance. Further progress towards better price stability may therefore be slow and importantly depend on a successful implementation of the government's anti-inflation programme and an improved productivity performance.

Part I of the present Survey reviews developments during the second recovery year against the background of previous cyclical experience. The reasons for the persistently high rate of unemployment and the rather hesitant growth of business fixed investment are examined in Part II analysing their medium-run implications for growth and full employment prospects. Part III is devoted to a discussion of recent economic policies and the present policy stance including the assumptions underlying the Secretariat's short-term outlook as presented in Part IV. The main conclusions that follow from this analysis are drawn in Part V.

I DEVELOPMENTS DURING THE SECOND RECOVERY YEAR

In terms of output growth, the now two years' old recovery has been well above previous post-war upturns (Diagram 1). However, since the starting point was unusually low, the margin of unemployed resources has remained much higher than at similar stages of previous post-war cycles: in the first quarter of 1977, eight quarters after the trough, real GNP was only $4\frac{3}{4}$ per cent above the previous peak, compared with an average gain of 9 per cent during the four previous upswings, the rate of capacity utilisation in manufacturing was only 81 per cent against an average of 84 per cent in earlier recoveries; and unemployment, at $7\frac{1}{2}$ per cent, was $2\frac{1}{4}$-3 percentage points higher than typical at this stage of the cycle. Despite the low degree of resource utilisation, inflation—as in most other countries—has remained comparatively high as inflationary expectations have subsided only slowly. Even so, an appreciable deceleration in the rate of price and wage increases has taken place in conditions of falling unemployment, possibly suggesting that the earlier deterioration in the inflation-unemployment trade-off has been partially reversed (Diagram 2).

Diagram 1   Comparison of cyclical recoveries

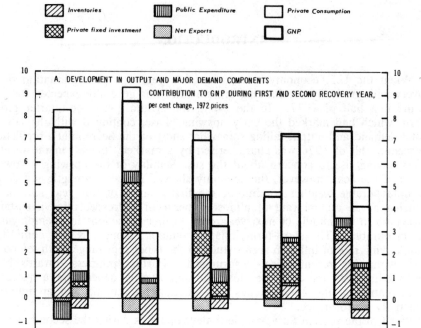

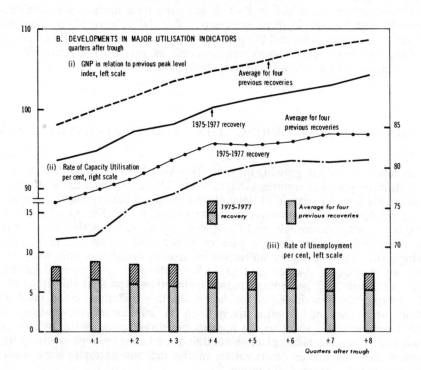

Diagram 2 **Major economic performance indicators**

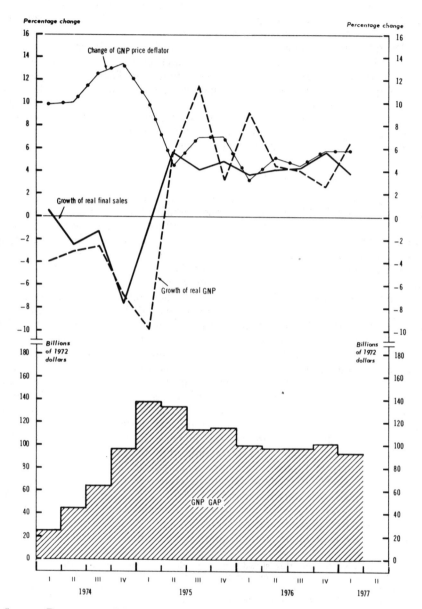

Sources: Department of Commerce, *Survey of Current Business,* and Council of Economic Advisers.

Another feature of the present recovery has been the very erratic growth pattern of output (Table 1), reflecting essentially large fluctuations in inventory formation, and the large deterioration in the external balance (Table 4). Thus the "pause" in the recovery in mid-1976 was heavily influenced by a levelling-off and subsequent decline in stockbuilding, though a temporary weakening in final demand also contributed to the slowdown in output growth[1]. Towards the end of the year, however, final demand—notably private consumption and residential construction—re-emerged as a strong source of buoyancy. This development led to a large and partly involuntary decline in inventory formation, reducing stock/final sales ratios to historically very low levels and setting the stage for a strong expansion of output. Consequently, the first quarter of this year saw a marked acceleration in output growth, as continued strength in final demand, coinciding with a sharp recovery of inventory formation, raised total domestic demand by almost 12 per cent (annual rate). Since, however, the rapid increase in demand was accompanied by a steep rise in imports—partly as a result of an unusually high fuel consumption during the winter—and exports fell, the trade balance deficit widened to more than $25 billion (annual rate).

Developments in domestic demand

Led by purchases of durable goods—particularly automobiles and parts—private consumption had been the main expansionary force during the initial phase of the upturn. In line with previous cyclical patterns, the contribution to overall growth declined during the second recovery year[2] with less buoyant household spending accentuating the mid-year "pause". Nevertheless, the propensity to consume has remained a good deal stronger than during previous upturns as the deceleration in the rate of growth was almost entirely due to a weaker trend of real income gains. Indeed, despite continued high rates of unemployment and inflation, the advance in household spending exceeded that of real disposable income, and by early 1977 the personal saving rate had fallen to less than 5 per cent, significantly below its long-term trend rate (Diagram 3)[3]. Apart from special and temporary factors (see Part IV) the strength and pattern of consumption has probably been influenced by the rather marked increase in participation rates for women in recent years and the longer-term trend towards smaller families. Hence, even though real disposable income per worker has shown only a moderate gain during the present upturn (see below), the advance in real income per household has probably been more in line with developments during previous cycles.

As further analysed in Part II, the increase in business fixed investment has so far remained rather modest, mainly due to excess capacity in many industries, a widespread move to improve corporate liquidity, but also as a consequence of uncertainties about the future course of the economy and government policies relating to environmental regulations and energy. On the other hand the recovery in residential construction, though coming later than in most previous cycles, has proved unexpectedly strong. With a spectacular gain of more than 35 per cent in the fourth quarter, residential investment for 1976 as

---

1 It is conceivable that this slowdown was related to the development in inventories as the large swing in the stock cycle and the resulting erratic growth pattern probably had an adverse impact on confidence in the private sector. Thus, fears of a reacceleration of inflation during periods of rapidly advancing output and rising budget deficits have alternated with doubts as to the sustainability of the upturn during periods of marked slowing down, inducing much uncertainty in the private sector and a related cautious spending behaviour.

2 In each of the post-war recoveries a "lull" in consumer spending has tended to occur 4-5 quarters after the trough, probably reflecting some catching-up on purchases of durable goods during the early phase of the recovery and a subsequent downward adjustment of household spending to the trend of disposable income. In this context it may be noted that the slowdown in spending was particularly sharp for durable goods, as the contribution to GNP growth fell by a full percentage point, from the first to the second recovery year.

3 Reflecting the strength of consumer confidence as well as the weakening trend for disposable income, outstanding instalment credit rose more than 11 per cent during the year ending in the first quarter of 1977, and the ratio of consumer credit to disposable income regained the longer-term trend of 16½ per cent. However, the repayment burden is still low and well below the average for the 1965-1974 period.

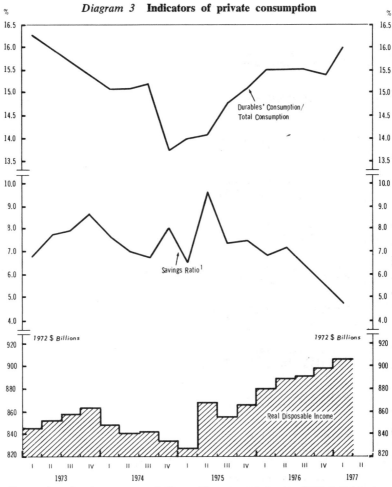

Diagram 3 **Indicators of private consumption**

1 Personal saving in per cent of disposable personal income (US definition).
Source: Department of Commerce, *Survey of Current Business.*

a whole rose more than 20 per cent and despite disruptive effects of the unusually cold weather early this year construction activity was running only 20 per cent below its previous unsustainably high peak. The recovery was particularly strong in the area of single family units, with housing starts regaining earlier peak rates by the end of 1976. Starts of rental units, on the other hand, have been less buoyant as comparatively high, though falling, vacancy rates and rent controls—or fear of their extension—have dampened investment incentives. A major factor behind the unexpectedly strong recovery in residential construction has no doubt been the easing of credit market conditions (Part III). Thus, the decline in short-term market interest rates has encouraged savings flows into thrift institutions, and the decline in long-term rates has stimulated demand for housing, even though rates have remained high by past standards[4].

4 It should be noted that despite the spectacular increase in residential investment in 1976, the net addition to the total housing stock was less than 1½ per cent and below the increase of the population of age 22 years and over.

Table 1   Demand and output

Percentage volume changes, seasonally adjusted annual rates

| | Annual | | | 1975 | | | | 1976 | | | | 1977 |
	1974	1975	1976	Q1	Q2	Q3	Q4	Q1	Q2	Q3	Q4	Q1
Personal consumption	−1.1	1.5	5.6	3.5	7.0	4.1	4.5	8.9	4.0	3.6	7.0	7.0
Government purchases	1.5	1.8	1.2	0.3	3.1	5.2	4.3	−4.9	2.6	2.9	−0.3	−4.3
Private fixed investment	−9.0	−13.7	8.7	−25.2	−6.3	6.4	7.7	11.8	10.3	11.1	10.3	12.1
Non-residential	−1.9	−13.3	3.9	−22.2	−12.6	−1.8	1.5	7.8	8.4	9.4	1.4	15.8
Residential	−24.6	−14.7	22.5	−34.2	16.8	34.1	25.3	22.7	15.3	15.7	35.1	4.0
Final domestic demand	−1.8	−0.7	5.0	−1.6	4.4	4.6	4.9	6.1	4.5	4.4	5.9	5.2
Inventory investment[1]	−0.5	−1.7	1.7	−10.0	0.1	7.0	−1.6	5.2	0.2	−0.3	−2.9	2.6
Total domestic demand	−2.4	−2.4	6.8	−10.8	4.2	12.2	3.3	11.8	4.7	4.0	2.8	7.9
Net exports[1]	0.7	0.5	−0.6	0.8	1.5	−0.5	0.3	−2.1	−0.2	−0.1	0.0	−0.9
Exports	11.2	−6.7	6.0	−21.4	−11.0	14.4	14.9	−1.3	7.9	11.4	−2.4	3.3
Imports	1.0	−15.7	17.7	−35.1	−33.5	31.6	18.2	39.9	13.1	15.4	−2.4	19.9
GNP	−1.7	−1.8	6.1	−9.9	5.6	11.4	3.3	9.2	4.4	3.9	2.6	6.9

1 Change as per cent of GNP of previous period, annual rate.

Source: Department of Commerce, Survey of Current Business.

The behaviour of inventories during this upturn has deviated markedly from earlier patterns, as the time lag with which changes in stocks typically follow the general business cycle has been much longer than earlier. This can essentially be explained by a considerable degree of "overshooting" during the recession and the early phase of the recovery and a subsequently more cautious behaviour on the part of firms:

(*i*) speculative motives combined with underestimation of the severity and length of the decline in sales meant that inventories continued to rise during most of the 1973-1975 recession. As a result, the inventory/sales ratio rose to a historically high level (Diagram 4), setting in motion a massive liquidation of stocks in the early phase of the recovery. Positive inventory formation was not resumed until one year after the recession trough[5] but doubts about the strength of the upturn kept stock formation quite low in relation to the pace of output, and the inventory/sales ratio continued to fall;

(*ii*) when this trend was reversed in the second half of 1976, firms, underestimating the strength in future sales, took steps to curtail inventories, even though the stock/sales ratio was rather low by past standards[6]. Consequently, when final demand accelerated in late 1976 and early this year, stocks/sales ratios fell to very low levels probably entailing a considerable degree of involuntary rundown of inventories.

In spite of the late recovery of stocks, inventory formation has had a marked positive impact on total output, accounting for about one-third of the rate of growth of GNP during the first four quarters of the present recovery. Since most of this was of a once-and-for-all nature, it was generally expected that inventory formation in the second recovery year would yield a much smaller, though still positive contribution to growth. However, due to the stumbling of the economy in the second half of 1976 and despite some strengthening early this year, the stock cycle had a negative influence on the rate of growth of total output, particularly in the final quarter of last year, when stock formation (1972 prices, annual rate) fell to only $ 0.9 billion, compared with $ 10.8 billion for the first half of the year.

Employment and productivity trends

The sharp rise in employment, which characterised developments during the early phase of the recovery, became even more pronounced during the year ending in March 1977, as the advance in the number of persons employed accelerated to almost 3 per cent. Due to sharp fluctuations in output and productivity developments, the employment gains have been rather unevenly distributed, with particularly strong increases during the first half of 1976 and in the first quarter of this year[7]. During the "pause", on the other hand, the rise in the number of persons employed fell below that of the total population but this trend was sharply reversed in the first quarter of this year when employment rose at an annual rate of 4 per cent. Recent

---

5 The turnaround in inventories occurred two quarters after the general recession trough, while earlier cycles normally have seen shorter lags.

6 The downward adjustment of inventory formation during the second half of 1976 was entirely due to changes in stocks of raw materials and finished goods, while manufacturers' work-in-process inventories actually showed a marked rise following a flat trend earlier in the year.

7 Due to the seasonal adjustment procedure currently used, employment may be slightly overestimated for the first halves of 1976 and 1977.

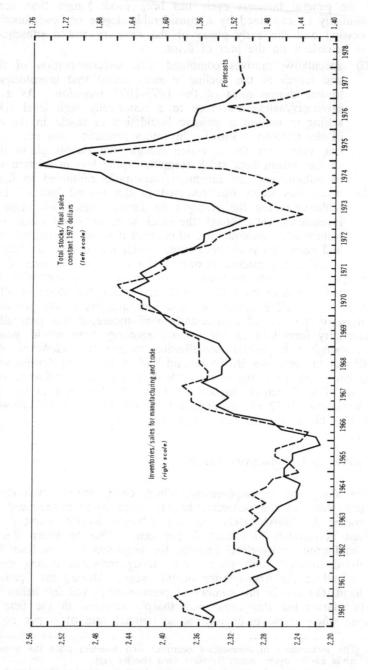

Diagram 4 **Inventory/sales ratios**

Total stocks/final sales
constant 1972 dollars
(left scale)

Forecasts

Inventories/sales for manufacturing and trade
(right scale)

developments have also shown a marked change in the sectoral distribution of employment gains: while during most of 1976 the rise in employment in the service producing sectors has exceeded that of the goods producing sectors, the year ending in April, 1977 showed employment in the latter rising at 3.2 per cent, compared with 2.9 per cent for the private sector as a whole.

Since the strong gain in employment was matched by an equally sharp rise in the labour force, the average rate of unemployment changed only little during the second year of recovery (see Part II). At the same time, the marked rise in the employment-output elasticity was tantamount to a significant decline in productivity advance. Measured as output per man-hour in the private non-farm sector, the rate of productivity increase for the year ending in the first quarter of 1977—though remaining well above the long-term trend rate— was only 2.4 per cent (compared with 5.7 per cent for the previous four quarters) with an actual fall in the last quarter of 1976. While productivity gains during the present recovery have been only slightly below those of previous cyclical upturns output per man-hour has risen only little relative to the pre-recession level, possibly suggesting that the extraordinary productivity decline in 1973-1974 was not just temporary. However, as discussed in Part II, there is evidence of a longer-term decline in the rate of productivity increase, and it is empirically difficult to disentangle such changes from the short-run cyclical fluctuations.

Wages and prices

Despite the very high rate of unemployment, average hourly earnings, though decelerating relative to 1975, increased by some 7 per cent last year (Table 2); total hourly compensation[8] went up even more as social security taxes were raised early in 1976. This apparent "stickiness" of wage increases in the face of a persistently large margin of slack may give the impression that, since the beginning of the 1970s, wages have become less responsive to changes in general demand conditions, making stabilisation policies less effective in slowing the rate of inflation[9]. However, price and wage developments over the past 3-4 years have been importantly influenced by supply constraints (food, feed, and fuel) and other special factors (termination of price-wage controls) which were largely unrelated to the overall level of demand. Moreover, recent empirical studies[10] taking specific account of the impact of past price increases and structural changes in the labour market, suggest that the short-run response of wages to changing employment conditions may have remained as strong as in the past:

    (*i*)   as further discussed in Part II, the composition of the labour force has changed significantly in recent years, implying that a given measured rate of unemployment is now associated with a smaller degree of labour market slack than earlier. Consequently, when related to unemployment rates adjusted for structural changes, recent wage developments are less out of line with past patterns. Moreover, judging by

---

    8 Compensations include supplements to wages and salaries and represent total labour costs to the employers.

    9 While in the 1950s and 1960s the rise in compensation per man-hour decelerated sharply after a cyclical peak, the four quarters following the peaks in 1969, Q4 and 1973, Q4 saw an acceleration of wage increases.

    10 See Perry, George L., "Changing Labour Markets and Inflation", *Brookings Papers on Economic Activity*, 3: 1970, pp. 411-41; Gordon, Robert J., "The Impact of Aggregate Demand on Prices", *Brookings Papers on Economic Activity*, 3: 1975, pp. 613-70 and Wachter, Michael L., "The Changing Cyclical Responsiveness of Wage Inflation" *Brookings Papers on Economic Activity*, 1: 1976, pp. 115-67.

the estimated slope of the "Phillips curve" there is little evidence of any decline in the responsiveness of wages to general demand conditions;

(*ii*) while the appropriate specification of the relationship between wage changes and labour market conditions is subject to a great deal of uncertainty, it is generally recognised that price changes (normally lagged) should be included to reflect catch-up effects induced by past price changes and/or the impact of inflationary expectations[11]. Consequently the apparent "stickiness" of nominal wage trends could be interpreted as a price-induced shift in the traditional "Phillips curve": in past recessions and during the early phase of recoveries rising unemployment rates have usually coincided with a decelerating rate of price inflation; however, during the most recent recession and subsequent recovery unemployment rates rose to unprecedented high levels with past very high rates of price inflation pushing up wage claims.

This relationship was clearly evident in 1975, when the first-year wage increases embodied in current settlements fell by two percentage points relative to 1974, but accelerating contributions from past wage settlements and particularly escalator provisions prevented total wage increases from decelerating by more than $\frac{3}{4}$ percentage point. As the impact of past price and wage developments gradually declined, this retarding factor lost importance in 1976 and the dampening impact of weak labour market conditions was clearly observable on first-year as well as total wage changes. Indeed, even though 1976 was a heavy bargaining year[12] and labour market conditions improved rather than deteriorated, the year-on-year advance in hourly earnings decelerated by as much as 2 percentage points. Consequently, when adjusted for structural changes in the labour force and the influence of past price increases, recent wage behaviour appears less out of line with previous trends. While the elimination of special price factors (see below) makes it difficult to draw any firm conclusions with respect to the unemployment-inflation trade-off, this development may suggest that the earlier outward shifts of the traditional "Phillips curve" have been partially reversed.

Despite the moderation in hourly wages and compensations, the rise in unit labour costs accelerated to 4 per cent during 1976 as the high rates of productivity growth typical of early cyclical phases subsided somewhat. Nevertheless, the rise in prices slowed down appreciably as special factors exerted a dampening influence:

(*i*) reflecting strong expansion in agricultural output, food prices at virtually all stages of production fell in 1976, particularly in the early part of the year;

(*ii*) gasoline and fuel prices also declined in early 1976 partly due to the impact of the Energy Policy and Conservation Act[13] and partly since supply exceeded demand, notably in major fuel consuming regions.

Measured by the implicit GNP deflator, the rate of inflation fell to 4.6 per cent during 1976 compared with 7.6 per cent during the preceding four quarters[14], while the moderation in consumer prices—from 7.0 to 4.8 per cent—was slightly less pronounced.

---

11 It should be noted, however, that if prices are mainly determined by wages (current and lagged) and general demand conditions, the inclusion of price changes into the wage equation is merely another way of saying that wages respond to changes in labour market conditions with a considerable time lag.

12 $4\frac{1}{2}$ million workers were under major contracts expiring during 1976.

13 This Act initially reduced the price of energy through a rollback of the ceiling on domestic crude oil prices and an abolition of the import fee.

14 Measured on a year-on-year basis the increase in the GNP deflator declined from 9.3 per cent in 1975 to 5.1 per cent in 1976.

Table 2 **Wages and prices**

Seasonally adjusted annual rates of change

	1974	1975	1976	1975 Q1	1975 Q2	1975 Q3	1975 Q4	1976 Q1	1976 Q2	1976 Q3	1976 Q4	1977 Q1
Wages:												
Average hourly earnings index	8.2	9.0	7.1	8.6	7.3	8.7	8.3	6.4	5.7	7.2	6.6	8.5
Compensation per man-hour (private non-farm)	9.5	9.6	7.4	11.4	7.1	6.5	5.7	9.1	7.8	7.0	7.1	10.2
Major collective bargaining settlements (first year change)	9.8	10.2	8.4	12.1	9.0	9.7	11.0	9.7	8.2	9.6	7.1	7.6
Prices:												
GNP deflator	10.0	9.3	5.1	10.1	4.5	7.0	7.1	3.2	5.2	4.4	5.8	5.8
Personal consumption deflator	10.8	8.0	5.1	6.4	4.6	7.2	5.8	3.8	4.4	5.3	5.5	6.7
Food	15.3	8.2	1.9	6.7	2.1	10.0	2.6	-1.7	1.1	1.4	1.4	7.5
Fuel oil and coal	59.0	8.3	7.3	-11.7	7.5	26.7	15.2	-8.8	2.8	17.5	11.6	22.5
Consumer price index	11.0	9.2	5.7	8.7	6.2	8.0	7.6	5.2	4.9	5.7	4.3	8.4
Wholesale price index	18.8	9.3	4.6	-0.7	3.4	7.2	7.8	1.2	5.1	3.4	6.4	8.6
Food and farm products	11.5	3.9	-0.6	-16.7	5.2	14.1	2.4	-12.3	8.4	7.9	-2.3	16.2
Industrial commodities	22.1	11.6	6.3	6.5	2.8	4.6	9.9	6.1	4.3	6.8	9.0	6.6

Sources: Department of Commerce, Survey of Current Business; Department of Labor, Monthly Labor Review.

However, a number of factors clearly suggest that the improved price performance was mostly temporary and not a reflection of a lower underlying rate of inflation. Indeed, the trend of the wholesale price index for industrial commodities steepened slightly as more moderate advances for finished goods were more than offset by accelerating prices for crude and intermediate non-food materials[15]. Moreover, the pattern of quarterly movements of non-food prices suggested that producers, with a time-lag, raised profit margins in line with improving demand conditions, with the "pause" mainly leading to postponement of further price increases and/or temporarily higher discounts[16]. Consequently, when the dampening effect from food and energy prices was reversed during the cold spell in early 1977, the rise in the fixed weighted GNP deflator accelerated to more than 5.6 per cent during the year to the first quarter of 1977, with the acceleration in consumer prices being even more pronounced.

The development in wage rates and consumer prices led to a rise in real hourly earnings (private non-farm economy) of $1\frac{3}{4}$ per cent between 1975 and 1976. While this was somewhat faster than the gains recorded a year earlier, the level of real earnings by the end of 1976 was still more than $1\frac{1}{2}$ per cent below the earlier peak; and despite the sharp rise in employment, total compensation of employees in per cent of national income has remained largely unchanged. At the same time, the share of before-tax corporate earnings rose $1\frac{1}{2}$ percentage points, as wider profit margins[17] and increasing sales volume combined to raise aggregate profits by almost 30 per cent. However, strongly influenced by the disruptive effects of the cold weather, this trend weakened in the first quarter of this year causing a probably temporary decline in the profit share[18].

Foreign trade and balance of payments

External transactions during the current upturn have exerted a growing contractionary influence. Reflecting the joint effect of a surge in imports related to the fast recovery of the U.S. economy and only a moderate expansion of exports, the fall in net exports (NIA basis, 1972 prices) reduced the rate of growth of GNP by almost $\frac{1}{2}$ percentage point during the year ending in the first quarter of 1977, compared with a negative growth contribution of approximately $\frac{1}{4}$ percentage point during the first year of recovery. Measured in current prices, this development has led to an unexpectedly large deterioration in the trade balance, which for 1976 was equivalent to 1 per cent of GNP. Following a surplus of $9 billion in 1975, the first quarter of 1976 saw a swing into deficit, which gradually widened in the course of the second year of recovery, reaching the record high rate of $27\frac{1}{2}$ billion (annual rate) in the first quarter of 1977.

This development can be related to three main factors (Table 3):

    (i)   the recovery of economic activity, accompanied by a large shift in inventory formation which has a relatively high import content, together

---

15   The acceleration was particularly sharp for crude materials, as prices rose 13.5 per cent during 1976 compared with only 4.5 per cent in 1975.

16   The development in steel prices clearly illustrates the influence of demand conditions. Reflecting increased demand from producers of consumer durables, prices of steel mill products were raised in the spring. However, as steel demand weakened during the summer, a price increase for sheet and strip products scheduled for October was rescinded due to widespread discounting and higher prices were not announced before late in the fourth quarter, when demand picked up again.

17   The ratio between prices and unit labour costs advanced $2\frac{3}{4}$ per cent in manufacturing, and by the end of the year after-tax corporate profits per unit of sales were 40 per cent above the rate recorded in the trough quarter.

18   Part II discusses alternative measures of profits and their implication for the rate of return on capital, noting in particular the importance of inflation adjustments in recent years and the rising share of interest payments on external debt.

with a reversal of the import shortfall of 1975 produced an increase in non-fuel imports which was more than twice the rise in industrial output;

(*ii*)   the gradual decline in domestic production of oil combined with a strong rise in domestic consumption and some speculative build-up of stocks towards the end of the year pushed up fuel imports by almost 23 per cent, following a virtually flat trend between 1974 and 1975;

(*iii*) since the United States was leading the world recovery in 1976, the development in export markets was considerably less buoyant than that of domestic demand for foreign products, particularly exports to non-oil LDC's which fell throughout most of 1976. In addition, the pronounced weakness of business fixed investment in virtually all major trading partners meant that the commodity composition of the recovery of export markets was unfavourable to U.S. industries, as exports of capital equipment normally account for 40 per cent of non-agricultural exports. As a result, non-agricultural exports (in volume) rose by less than 1 per cent, compared with an overall market growth of 7½ per cent.

Table 3   **Merchandise trade, terms of trade and effective exchange rate movements**

	1975	1976	1977[2]	1975 H. 2	1976 H. 1	1976 H. 2	1977[2] H. 1	1977[2] H. 2	1978[2] H. 1
				$ billion, current prices, actual rates					
Exports[1]	107.1	114.7	127.9	54.2	55.4	59.3	61.5	66.4	70.5
Agricultural	22.2	23.4		11.3	11.2	12.3			
Non-agricultural	84.8	91.3		42.9	44.2	47.0			
Imports[1]	98.1	123.9	152.4	49.9	58.2	65.7	74.8	77.6	82.2
Fuel	28.5	37.1		14.9	17.0	20.2			
Non-fuel	69.6	86.8		35.0	41.2	45.7			
Trade balance	9.0	−9.2	−24.5	4.3	−2.8	−6.4	−13.3	−11.2	−11.7
				Per cent change, SAAR (1975 = 100)					
Exports									
Volumes	−2.7	3.6	4¼	11.1	−1.6	7.1	0	10	6½
Average values	12.5	3.4	6	−1.4	4.8	5.5	6	6	5½
Imports									
Volumes	−12.2	21.5	14	12.9	26.0	21.4	16	4	6½
Average values	8.4	30	9	−6.0	6.3	5.9	11½	7	5
				Indices					
Terms of trade	100.0	100.4	97.6	101.1	100.5	100.3	97.8	97.4	97.6
Effective exchange Rate (1970, Q1 = 100)	84.0	87.6		86.5	87.6	87.6			

1   Balance-of-payments basis.
2   Secretariat forecast.
Sources: Federal Reserve System, *Federal Reserve Bulletin*, April 1977 and OECD Secretariat.

While the above factors taken together would have reduced the trade balance by more than $22 billion between 1975 and 1976, the actual deterioration was somewhat less, due to a marked rise in agricultural exports (almost 12 per cent in volume) and a small gain in the terms of trade (around ½ per cent). Moreover, only part of the swing in the trade balance was reflected in the current account (Table 4). Net investment income—mainly as a result of higher receipts from direct investments and larger returns on securities and bank loans—showed an increase of $4½ billion, and for the first time ever net military transactions were in surplus. Consequently, the current account was largely in balance in 1976, following a surplus of almost $12 billion the previous year[19].

About half of the corresponding swing in the capital account from a net outflow in 1975 to a small inflow in 1976 was accounted for by unrecorded transactions and appeared as a rise in the "statistical discrepancy". The main factor behind the recorded shift in capital flows was a substantial rise in foreign official funds placed in the United States. From a level of $7 billion, this inflow rose to more than $18 billion in 1976, with most of the increase being accounted for by a build-up of reserves held by Japan. The increase of OPEC official assets, though amounting to almost half of the recorded inflow of official funds, was only moderately higher than that registered in 1975[20]. On the other hand, U.S. government transactions—including changes in official reserves—led to a larger capital outflow than in 1975, and private capital market transactions also left a higher deficit since the marked decline in the net flow of foreign lending by U.S. banks[21], was more than offset by a sharp rise in foreign bond flotations in the U.S. market[22].

While the large swing in the balance of payments had a relatively small direct effect on the U.S. economy[23] nor any bearing on policies, its impact on other Member countries and LDC's was important, though somewhat unevenly distributed. Thus, the trade surplus vis-à-vis non-OPEC countries declined by $11½ billion between 1975 and 1976 of which shifts in the trade balance with Japan and Canada accounted for almost 50 per cent, corresponding to 1 and 1¼ per cent of GNP in the two respective countries. On the other hand, the trade surplus with Western Europe remained unchanged, reflecting partly a large increase in agricultural exports to countries adversely affected by the drought and partly the longer lags with which a recovery in the United States affects the economies of Western Europe.

---

19 Despite the cyclical swing in the current account, the trade-weighted exchange value of the $ appreciated 4½ per cent during 1976.

20 It should be noted that part of the rise in the "statistical discrepancy" may reflect unrecorded capital inflows from OPEC countries.

21 At $10 billion, however, the outflow of bank-reported private capital has remained high by past standards, which, apart from the abandonment of official controls on capital flows since January, 1974, probably reflected weak domestic demand for credit as well as a strong foreign demand related to the general rise in balance-of-payments deficits of other Member countries.

22 Reflecting a rather wide interest rate differential, Canada was the largest foreign borrower with total new bond placement amounting to $5.2 billion or $2 billion more than in 1975.

23 Even including multiplier effects, the impact of changes in net exports (NIA basis, 1972 prices) is unlikely to have exceeded ¾ of one per cent of GNP.

Table 4 **Balance of payments**
$ Billion, seasonally adjusted, actual rates

	1974	1975	1976	1977[3]	1976 H.1	1976 H.2	1977[3] H.1	1977[3] H.2	1978[3] H.1
Current account									
Merchandise exports	98.3	107.1	114.7	128.9	55.4	59.3	61.2	67.2	71.5
Merchandise imports	103.7	98.1	123.9	149.1	58.2	65.7	72.6	76.5	81.4
Trade balance	−5.4	9.0	−9.2	−24.5	−2.8	−6.4	−13.3	−11.2	−11.7
Military transactions, net	−2.1	−0.9	0.4		0.2	0.6			
Investment income, net	10.2	6.0	10.5	10.5	4.8	5.7	5.3	5.2	5.2
Other service transactions, net	0.9	2.3	7.7		1.2	1.5			
Unilateral transfers	−7.2	−4.6	−5.0		−2.0	−3.0			
Balance on current account	−3.6	11.8	−0.6	−14.0	1.0	−1.6	−8.0	−6.0	−6.5
Capital account[1]									
Private capital, net									
Direct investment	−5.0	−3.9	−4.4		−2.3	−2.1			
Security transactions	−0.8	−1.0	−4.6		−2.8	−1.8			
Claims reported by banks, net	−3.5	−12.8	−9.8		−4.2	−5.6			
Others, net	−1.6	−1.4	−2.4		−1.9	−0.5			
US Government, net[2]	0.4	−3.5	−4.3		−1.7	−2.6			
Foreign official assets in the US	11.0	6.9	18.1		8.0	10.1			
of which: OPEC countries	10.0	7.1	9.5		6.8	2.7			
Official reserves	−1.4	−0.6	−2.5		−2.3	−0.2			
Statistical discrepancy	4.6	4.6	10.5		6.2	4.3			

1 (+) = inflow, (—) = outflow.
2 Excluding change in official reserves.
3 Secretariat forecast.
Sources: Department of Commerce, *Survey of Current Business* 1977 and earlier, Federal Reserve System, *Federal Reserve Bulletin*, April 1977 and OECD Secretariat.

II THE GROWTH OF POTENTIAL OUTPUT: PROBLEMS AND PROSPECTS

After two years of recovery, certain important activity indicators have remained at levels usually associated with recessions. The two prominent examples are the continued high rate of unemployment (despite a strong growth of employment), and the hesitant growth of business fixed investment (despite the strong recovery of profits and the restoration of corporate liquidity that have taken place since the recession). The following paragraphs examine these two features, tracing their basic roots, and analysing their implications for the longer-run development of the economy, in general, and for the growth of productive potential, in particular.

Labour market developments

Throughout 1976, unemployment remained stubbornly resistant to the relatively strong growth in output. After falling from the recession high of 9 per cent in May 1975 to 7.3 per cent by May 1976, the unemployment rate started to creep up again, reaching 8 per cent by November. Apart from the mid-year "pause" and above-average rates of productivity increases, this was due mainly to the unusually rapid growth of the labour force, rising at an average annual rate of over 3 per cent in the first three quarters of 1976. However, the subsequent deceleration of labour force growth (down to 1¾ per cent annually in the last quarter of 1976 and the first quarter of 1977) combined with a slower advance of productivity to produce a large reduction in labour market slack in the first quarter of 1977[24] and by May the unemployment rate was down to 6.9 per cent.

A sharp rise in the labour force is of course quite normal in a cyclical upswing, as the availability of more jobs entices secondary workers back into the labour force. The data on "discouraged workers", though, indicate that this normal cyclical pattern was not the main explanation for the very rapid increase experienced during 1976[25]. The main reason was rather that the

---

24 The factors underlying the movement in the unemployment rate may be seen from the table of annual growth rates (in per cent):

	Output	Output per man-hour	Man hours	Employment	Civilian labour force	Unemployment
1976 Q1	10.5	5.4	4.8	4.7	2.3	7.5
Q2	5.4	4.4	1.0	3.4	3.9	7.6
Q3	3.0	2.6	0.4	1.8	3.1	7.8
Q4	1.9	−1.2	3.2	2.1	1.9	7.9
1977 Q1	8.3	4.1	4.1	4.1	1.5	7.4

The first four columns refer to private non-agricultural business, the last two to the total civilian labour force.

Source: Bureau of Labor Statistics.

25 "Discouraged workers" are those who report, in the household employment survey, that they are not in the labour force for job market reasons: that is, they do not seek work because they are pessimistic about their chances of success. Between the final quarter of 1975 and the third quarter of 1976, the number of discouraged workers fell by 235 000. Since this explains only 10 per cent of the total increase in the labour force taking place during this period, it seems likely that the increase in the labour force reflected other than purely cyclical factors. However, the slow growth in the labour force in the final quarter of 1976 was largely due to the economic slowdown. The number of discouraged workers increased sharply: had these people stayed in the labour force, the growth rate would have been 2.9 per cent, rather than the actual 1.9 per cent. The comparatively slow growth of the labour force in the first quarter of 1977 is harder to explain since the number of discouraged workers actually fell; the cold weather may be part of the explanation.

potential labour force has been growing more rapidly in recent years than earlier (Table 8) largely because of an accelerated increase in the participation rate of women and, to a lesser extent, of teenagers. This long-standing trend has resulted in a steady increase over the past 20 years in the percentage of women in the labour force; somewhat less important, the teenage percentage has also gradually increased.

Since unemployment rates tend to be relatively high amongst women and teenagers, these changes in the composition of the labour force (and associated changes in the occupational structure) have raised the measured degree of labour market slack and affected the "full employment rate of unemployment" as well as the underlying rate of productivity growth. As can be seen from Table 5, the higher than average unemployment rates for women and particularly teenagers are to a large extent related to a large share of new entrants and re-entrants, symptomatic of a more unstable attachment to the labour market and possibly reflecting poor job opportunities[26]. Thus the unemployment rate for teenagers was as high as 19 per cent in 1976 of which two-thirds was accounted for by job-seekers either entering the labour force for the first time or otherwise re-entering it[27]. In addition, there has been, throughout this period, a secular tendency for the rate of teenage unemployment to increase, implying that a given pressure of demand in labour markets is now associated with a higher level of teenage unemployment than previously. These two developments—the changed composition of the labour force and higher teenage unemployment—largely explain why the full-employment unemployment rate is now generally assumed to be higher than before[28] [29].

Secondly, the more rapid growth of less skilled and lower-paid workers means that the "effective" labour force has been growing somewhat less rapidly than the actual labour force. Quantitative estimates of this are obviously uncertain but recalculating the latest quinquennial growth of the labour force in terms of equivalent adult male units yields a slightly lower growth rate[30]. Such a shift in the quality of the labour force may also have contributed to the deceleration in productivity growth.

---

26 The fact that more teenagers lose or leave their jobs than do other groups of workers (Table 5) may be a reflection of the lack of attractive job opportunities.

27 While these new or re-entrants usually do not remain unemployed for very long, it should also be noted that teenagers—particularly black youths—have more frequent spells of unemployment than adult male workers. Moreover, there is evidence that teenagers are more likely to end a spell of unemployment by withdrawing from the labour force. On the other hand, in assessing the problem of youth unemployment, it is important to note that a large share of young job seekers are only looking for part-time jobs.

28 The latest official estimate puts the "full-employment" unemployment rate at 4.9 per cent, compared with 4 per cent in 1955. See the *Economic Report of the President*, 1977, p. 51. This is also the estimate of George L. Perry of the Brookings Institution. See "Potential Output and Productivity" (forthcoming). Other estimates, though, put the rate as high as 5.5 per cent: see, for example, Michael L. Wachter, "The Changing Cyclical Responsiveness of Wage Inflation", *Brookings Papers on Economic Activity*, 1976:1.

29 It is important to note that the 4.9 per cent estimated by the outgoing Council of Economic Advisers is developed only on the basis of demographic characteristics of the labour force. The unemployment rate consistent with nonaccelerating inflation would probably be somewhat higher.

30 With the maturation of the "baby boom" generation and increased female participation rates, the actual growth in the labour force was 11.2 per cent between 1970 and 1975. As the new entrants tend to be less skilled and may have shorter working weeks, weekly earnings are lower than average. Reweighting each component of the labour force by its medium weekly earnings gives a growth rate of only 10.08 per cent (adult male equivalents). The difference could well be a reflection of changes in the composition of labour demand—from highly paid manufacturing jobs to less well-paid service sector jobs, for instance.

Table 5 **Unemployment rate by reason for unemployment, 1976**

	Both sexes 16-19	Male 20+	Female 20+	Total
Lost last job	4.3	4.1	3.2	3.8
Left last job	1.7	0.6	1.2	0.9
Re-entered labour force	5.5	1.0	2.6	2.0
Never worked before	7.5	0.2	0.4	0.9
Total	19.0	5.9	7.4	7.7
Memorandum item:				
High employment rate[1]	14.1	3.9	5.2	4.9

1 Estimated from Peter K. Clark, "A New Estimate of Potential GNP". (Council of Economic Advisers, 1977.)
   Source: Bureau of Labor Statistics.

Diagram 5 **Unemployment rates**
Per cent of the Civilian Labour Force

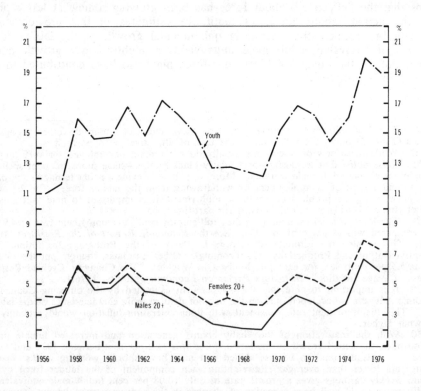

Source: Bureau of Labor Statistics, *Employment and Earnings.*

The productivity slowdown

During the last four years, output per man-hour (non-farm business sector) has been advancing at an average annual rate of less than 1 per cent, giving rise to concern about a possible trend deterioration of productivity growth. However, the interpretation of these developments is complicated by the fact that the last few years have been marked by a severe recession. According to econometric work undertaken by the Secretariat (the details are reported in Annex I), the underlying rate appears to have fallen from $2\frac{1}{2}$-$2\frac{3}{4}$ per cent per annum in the late 1950s to only $1\frac{3}{4}$ per cent per annum by the mid-1970s[31]. Furthermore, the productivity performance in the last four years was significantly depressed by the recession. On the basis of past cyclical movements, the yearly productivity advance would have fallen about one percentage point below its underlying trend for the 1973-1976 period. In the event, it fell 0.9 percentage point below (Table 6), closely in line with previous experience.

Table 6 **Productivity[1] performance in recent years**
Percentage change

	1973	1974	1975	1976	Average 1973-1976
Underlying rate	1.8	1.8	1.8	1.7	1.8
Rate due to cyclical factors	0.7	−4.1	−2.4	2.1	−1.0
Unexplained variation	−0.8	−1.2	2.4	0.2	0.1
	1.7	−3.5	1.8	3.6	0.9

1 Output per man-hour, non-farm business sector.
Sources: Bureau of Labor Statistics and Secretariat estimates (see Annex I).

Nonetheless, the actual growth of productivity in particular years deviated substantially from the rate suggested by earlier historical patterns. In 1974, the productivity fall was unusually sharp, probably because businessmen failed at the time to recognise the depth of the subsequent recession and did not lay off labour as quickly as output fell[32]. Indeed the process of shedding labour continued into 1975, as the recession bottomed out; by 1976, however, activity recovered rapidly, and output per man-hour registered the strong gains usually associated with the upswing phase of the trade cycle (Table 6).

Explaining the decelerating trend of productivity growth is more difficult. One important factor may be the gradual shift in the composition of the labour force in favour of less productive workers that was noted above. There is, in fact, evidence that hardly any deceleration can be detected when the different groups of the labour force are weighted according to their efficiencies, as

31 This estimate is close to that of the Council of Economic Advisers, who put the basic rate of productivity growth in recent years at 1.8 per cent per annum (*Economic Report of the President*, January, 1977, p. 54).

32 This interpretation is supported by businessmen's inventory policy at the time, when they continued piling up inventories even though final demand had weakened, presumably on the expectation of a rapid pick-up in demand. This explanation was also advanced at the time by Arthur Okun ("Unemployment and Output in 1974", *Brookings Papers on Economic Activity*, 1974:2).

measured by wage rates[33]. Thus the slowdown in the *aggregate* measure of productivity may *not* be due to a slower productivity gain of particular workers[34].

A second and possibly related factor is the development in the capital/labour ratio. According to official estimates, the rate of growth in effective capital per man-hour—after adjustment for cyclical factors—fell from some 3 per cent in the 1950s to around 2¾ per cent in the 1966-1973 period and to only 1¾ per cent over the last three years. Except for the most recent period, when the weakness of business fixed investment reduced the rate of growth of the capital stock, this decrease is mainly attributable to the faster increase in the labour supply, which has not been matched by higher capital spending. Moreover, higher obsolescence rates and rising expenditure on pollution abatement have probably meant that gross investment flows in the 1970s have added less to productive capacity than in earlier periods. But it is difficult to estimate to what extent the development in the capital/labour ratio has contributed to the trend decline in the rate of productivity increase[35], as changes in the composition of employment have influenced the aggregate capital/labour ratio[36].

Investment developments

The recent growth of the capital stock has been relatively weak: investment/GNP and investment/capital stock ratios are now low by the standards of the 1960s and early 1970s (Diagram 6). Investment activity has remained subdued even in absolute terms: in 1976 the volume of fixed non-residential investment was only a little higher than a decade earlier[37], and 10 per cent below the level attained in 1973 and 1974. Furthermore, the current recovery—now more than two years old—has produced a rise in investment expenditure that is clearly modest by earlier cyclical experience, an annual rate of only 3.2 per cent in the first two recovery years, compared with an average annual rate of 6.6 per cent for the previous three upturns[38]. This divergence is, though, largely attributable to the unusually severe decline during the recession combined with a longer-than-normal time lag between the general cyclical trough and the turning point of the investment cycle. Thus, when measured from the specific trough, the rate of growth of capital expenditure during the present recovery has been only marginally below that of previous cyclical upturns.

---

33 See George L. Perry, "Labour Force Structure, Potential Output, and Productivity". *Brookings Paper on Economic Activity*, 3:1971. He estimated that the rate of growth of output per man-hour fell from 2.7 per cent in the 1950s and early 1960s to 2.4 per cent by the second half of the 1960s, and that virtually all of this difference was due to shifts in the composition of employment (p. 552). Such shifts in the age/sex composition will doubtless reflect changes in the structure of labour demand and the differing age/sex composition of the various sectors.

34 In this context it is relevant to note that if the positive impact of increasing educational attainment is also taken into account only a fractional share of the slow down in productivity can be related to less efficient manhour inputs. Hence the slow down in labour productivity may be even more pronounced than meets the eye.

35 The Council of Economic Advisers has estimated that between one-tenth and one-third of the productivity slowdown since 1966 can be explained by slower growth in effective capital per man-hour. According to estimates made by the Congressional Budget Office, the contribution to productivity increases from the growth in capital per worker has fallen from 0.7-0.9 percentage points in the 1960s to 0.2-0.4 percentage points in the 1970s.

36 Trends in the capital/labour ratio show wide variations between sectors. In manufacturing recent growth rates are in line with earlier trends, while in the service sectors, which have absorbed the bulk of the increase in employment, growth rates have been falling.

37 In 1976 the volume of fixed non-residential investment was $115.7 billion (constant 1972 dollars), compared with an average of $108 billion for the period 1966 to 1969.

38 The increases were 7.0 per cent, 5.0 per cent, and 7.7 per cent for the recoveries starting in 1958, 1961 and 1970 respectively.

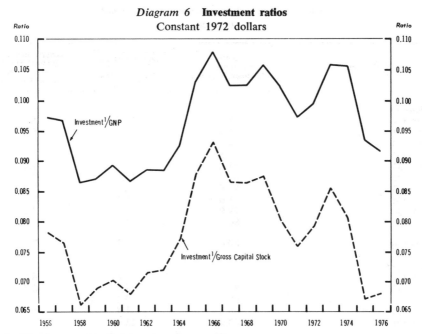

Diagram 6 **Investment ratios**
Constant 1972 dollars

1   Fixed non-residential investment expenditures.
Source: Department of Commerce, *Survey of Current Business.*

It is reasonable to assume that weak investment demand is related to the existence of relatively low rates of capacity utilisation, although how much this explains is uncertain.   Certainly there is no post-war precedent for the steep decline in capacity utilisation rates during the last recession[39].   For this reason, the capacity utilisation rates reached in the second recovery year were generally attained earlier in previous cycles.   Indeed, a simple comparison of recent quarters of the present recovery with those quarters in earlier recoveries with similar utilisation rates suggests that current investment behaviour is not so far out of line with earlier cycles.   During 1976 and the first quarter of 1977, real business fixed investment increased at an average annual rate of 8.6 per cent, almost exactly in line with previous experience[40] (Table 7).   However, this comparison may be misleading since the recent upturn in investment started from a relatively low level: expressed as a percentage of the capital stock, investment demand appears significantly weaker than in previous recoveries.   Had investment last year reached the rate of 7 per cent of the capital stock typical of previous recoveries (Table 7), the increase in investment expenditures between 1975 and 1976 would have been almost twice as large as it actually was[41].

39   The FRB's utilisation rate for manufacturing industry stood at 70.9 per cent in the first quarter of 1975 (the trough quarter of the last recession), compared with 72.4 in 1958 Q2, 73.8 in 1961 Q1 and 76.3 in 1970 Q4 (trough quarters of earlier cycles).
40   Investment in the fourth quarter of 1976 was probably depressed by the auto strike, as well as by the uncertainty generated by the "pause" in activity in the latter part of 1976, and by the Presidential election.   The strong first quarter performance was, partly at least, a "catch-up" from the abnormally depressed fourth quarter.
41   In 1976 real business fixed investment was up 3.9 per cent on the 1975 level: this compares with a 7.0 per cent increase had investment expenditure reached 7 per cent of the end-1975 capital stock.

Table 7 **Cyclical comparison of investment**
Per cent

Quarter	FRB Utilisation rate (All manufacturing)	Increase in gross fixed non-residential investment (annual rates 1972 dollars)	Quarterly investment (annual rates) as per cent of capital stock
Previous cycles[1]			
1958 Q4	78.2	12.5	6.5
1959 Q1	81.4	10.6	6.6
1961 Q3	78.4	2.5	6.7
Q4	80.6	12.8	6.9
1962 Q1	81.2	8.5	7.0
Q2	81.3	14.0	7.2
Q3	81.6	5.1	7.2
Q4	81.6	−4.9	7.1
1971 Q4	79.0	8.4	7.2
1972 Q1	80.9	14.2	7.7
Average	80.4	8.3	7.0
Present cycle			
1976 Q1	79.0	7.8	6.6
Q2	80.2	8.4	6.7
Q3	80.8	9.4	6.7
Q4	80.4	1.4	6.7
1977 Q1	80.9	15.8	
	80.3	8.6	

NOTE The first measure (quarter-to-quarter growth rates of fixed non-residential investment) can be misleading if based on quarters of an abnormally low level of investment. To minimise this problem, the second measure (fixed non-residential investment as a percentage of the capital stock) is also shown.

1 1958 Q4 and 1961 Q3 were the second quarters of the recovery; 1971 Q4 and 1976 Q1 were the fourth quarters of the recovery.

Sources: Board of Governors, Federal Reserve System, *Federal Reserve Bulletin* and Department of Commerce, *Survey of Current Business.*

Four factors are usually singled out as the most important determinants of investment behaviour: profitability; the composition of corporate balance sheets; costs of capital investment; and the general business outlook.

(i) *The rate of return*

Investment depends, among other things, on the expected future rate of return. Given the difficulty of quantifying such expected rates of return, data on *actual* profitability may provide some guidance. Considerable importance has been attached in recent years to the supposed secular decline, since the mid-1960s in corporate profitability. But a main problem is that the trend of profitability is very sensitive to the measure of profitability used, since the composition of gross cash flow[42] of the corporate sector has changed so markedly over the last twenty years (Diagram 8). Of the many measures of profitability, the declining share of profits in national income has perhaps attracted the greatest attention,

42 Gross cash flow for the non-financial corporate sector is defined as profits before tax (without the capital consumption adjustment and the inventory valuation adjustment) *plus* capital consumption allowances (also without the capital consumption adjustment) *plus* net interest *plus* foreign branch profits.

Diagram 7 **Measures of capacity utilisation**
Manufacturing Industry

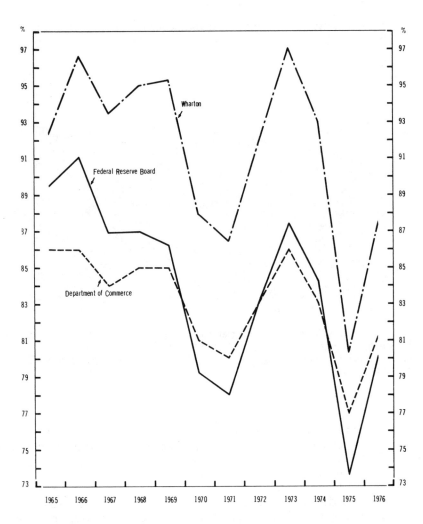

Sources: Wharton EFA, Board of Governors, Federal Reserve System, *Federal Reserve Bulletin* and Department of Commerce, *Survey of Current Business.*

and with reason: by 1976 after-tax profits (adjusted for inflation)—the measure that appears in the national accounts—was a little over 4 per cent of corporate GDP[43] (Diagram 8), whereas it rarely fell below 6 per cent in the late 1950s and 1960s. There are, however, two reasons for thinking that this shows an unduly beak picture of profitability developments:

   (a)   present accounting practices for financial assets/liabilities tend to under-
state profits in an inflationary environment, as the inflation adjustment

---

43   Figures refer to non-financial corporations.

Diagram 8 **Measures of profitability**
Non-financial corporations

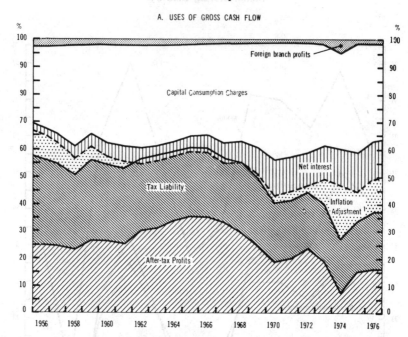

A. USES OF GROSS CASH FLOW

1   The inflation adjustment reflecting also changing tax laws is taken as the sum of the capital consumption adjustment and the inventory valuation adjustment.

Sources: Federal Reserve System, *Flow of Funds Accounts* and Department of Commerce, *Survey of Current Business.*

employed to reach NIA profits[44] does not take account of the reduction of the real value of money debt.   Though the magnitude of this gain is difficult to gauge, the sheer size of the non-financial corporate debt makes it likely to be large[45];

(b)   the declining share of profits in national income does not necessarily imply a declining trend in the returns to capital.   The reason for this is that much of the expansion of the corporate sector during the last 20 years has been financed by borrowing rather than internally (or by raising equity capital) so that the debt-equity ratio has gone

---

44   The inflation adjustment consists of putting capital consumption charges on a replacement cost basis and of subtracting the inflation gains on inventories.   The magnitude of this adjustment is substantial: it soared from a mere 2 per cent of gross cash flow in the mid-1950s to almost 20 per cent by 1974, the worst inflationary year, and has remained high by historical standards ever since (Diagram 8A).   Thus, up to 1972, net profits unadjusted and net profits adjusted for inflation moved closely together but have diverged sharply since then (Diagrams 8 B and 8 C).

45   Non-financial corporate debt was about $650 billion in 1976.   But the exact gain from inflation will depend on the term structure of this debt.   There is of course no inflationary gain from debt recently incurred at interest rates reflecting current rates of inflation. However, much of this debt was raised earlier at the low interest rates appropriate to earlier inflation rates, and the inflation gains on such debt are likely to be substantial.   This issue is discussed in detail by John B. Shoven and Jeremy I. Bulow ("Inflation Accounting and Non-financial Corporate Profits". *Brookings Papers on Economic Activity*, 1976:1).

Diagram 8 (Contd.) **Measures of profitability**
Non-financial corporations

B. AS A PERCENTAGE OF NET WORTH

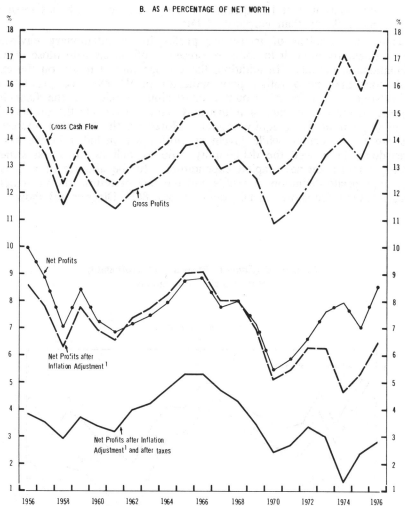

1   The inflation adjustment reflecting also changing tax laws is taken as the sum of the capital consumption adjustment and the inventory valuation adjustment.

Sources: Federal Reserve System, *Flow of Funds Accounts* and Department of Commerce, *Survey of Current Business.*

from little over a quarter in the mid-1950s to almost half by 1974. Consequently, a progressively greater part of the returns to corporate capital has accrued to outside debt holders, so that the net interest component of gross cash flow has risen sharply over the last 20 years from just under 3 per cent in 1956 to about 14 per cent by 1976 (Diagram 8)[46].   For much the same reason, profits expressed as a

46   This development also reflects increasing nominal rates of interest during the last 20 years.

percentage of corporate net worth have not fallen as sharply as profits in per cent of corporate GDP, since the increased corporate reliance on external debt has meant that corporate net worth has risen much more slowly than corporate GDP.

Thus, the problem of measuring profits in an inflationary environment makes it singularly difficult to compare present profit levels with those of earlier, less inflationary, periods. In addition, the average rate of return on the existing capital stock may be a rather poor indicator of the expected profitability of new investments. If firms encounter constraints in selecting the financing of new projects, the overall rate of return may tend to overstate the profitability of invested internal funds or equity capital. Moreover, the fact that interest payments are tax-deductible while inventory profits are included in the tax base has no doubt influenced the debt/equity ratio as well as firms' assessment of the rate of return on new capital expenditure. In the absence of a consensus on the appropriate definition of profits and the rate of return, the movements of various measures are shown in Diagrams 8B and 8C. Diagram 8B shows profits

Diagram 8 (Contd.) **Measures of profitability**
Non-financial corporations

C. AS A PERCENTAGE OF GDP

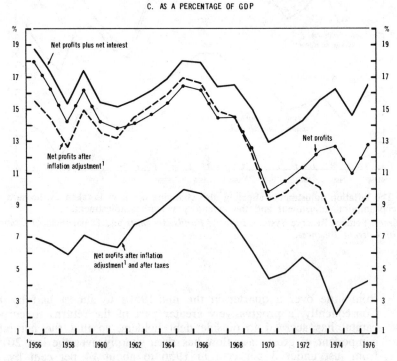

1   The inflation adjustment reflecting also changing tax laws is taken as the sum of the capital consumption adjustment and the inventory valuation adjustment.

Sources: Federal Reserve System, *Flow of Funds Accounts* and Department of Commerce, *Survey of Current Business.*

measured as the rate of return on net worth, while Diagram 8C shows the profit share of GDP[47].

(ii) *Restructuring balance sheets*

The rise in profits since the recession has served not only to raise the rate of return on investment, but also to improve the liquidity position of the non-financial sector, which was unusually squeezed in the last recession. Also, the severity of that recession may have made the dangers of increased reliance on external (especially short-term debt) financing more evident. For these reasons, some restructuring of corporate balance sheets was inevitable in the recovery, and the process of correction doubtless held back investment spending. A marked restructuring has indeed taken place, featuring the refunding of short-term debt with longer-term maturities, and assisted by the strong recovery in cash flow. Compared with earlier recoveries a greater part of the extra funds availabe to non-financial corporations was used to purchase financial assets, and a smaller part to finance fixed investment (Diagram 9). This was most marked in the last two quarters of 1975 when a very substantial rundown of inventories allowed a rapid accumulation of financial assets, with liquidity ratios returning to levels more normal by recent standards[48], a welcome development for many corporations after the scares of the last recession[49].

Secondly, the debt/equity ratio of the non-financial corporate sector actually fell in 1976, after 20 years of uninterrupted increase. The earlier tendency towards greater indebtedness reflects in part the fact that interest payments are an allowed deduction from profits for tax purposes, while dividends on equity are not. One problem of an increasing debt/equity ratio is that claims of fixed interest payments on cash flow grow larger. As this happens, the cyclical development of net cash flow (i.e. net of fixed claims such as interest payments) grows more volatile. The greater volatility of cash flow available for dividends (after deduction of interest payments, capital consumption allowances and taxes) may make it harder to raise equity finance, and may partly explain the weakness in the stock market during the last few years. This consideration—and more

---

47 The various measures of profits shown in the diagrams are defined as follows (1976 figures used for illustration):

	Per cent of gross cash flow [1]
Net profits after inflation adjustment and after taxes	16.2
plus tax liability *equals*	20.8
Net profits after inflation adjustment	37.1
plus inflation adjustment *equals*	11.7
Net profits	48.7
plus capital consumption allowances *equals*	35.6
Gross profits	84.4
plus net interest and	13.8
plus foreign branch profits *equals*	1.8
Gross cash flow	100.0

1 Totals may not add because of rounding.
Sources: Department of Commerce: *Survey of Current Business,* Federal Reserve Board: *Flow of Funds.*

48 But the liquidity position is still much weaker than it was in the 1950s and early 1960s.

49 Part of the liquidity improvement did, though, reflect certain special temporary influences: (*i*) the reduction of inventory formation at the end of 1976 and the shortfall of actual below intended investment expenditures; (*ii*) expectations in early 1976 of rising interest rates (though unjustified *ex post*) and (*iii*) the more rapid rise of profit tax liabilities than actual payments all contributed to the liquidity strengthening.

Diagram 9   Liquidity of non-financial corporations

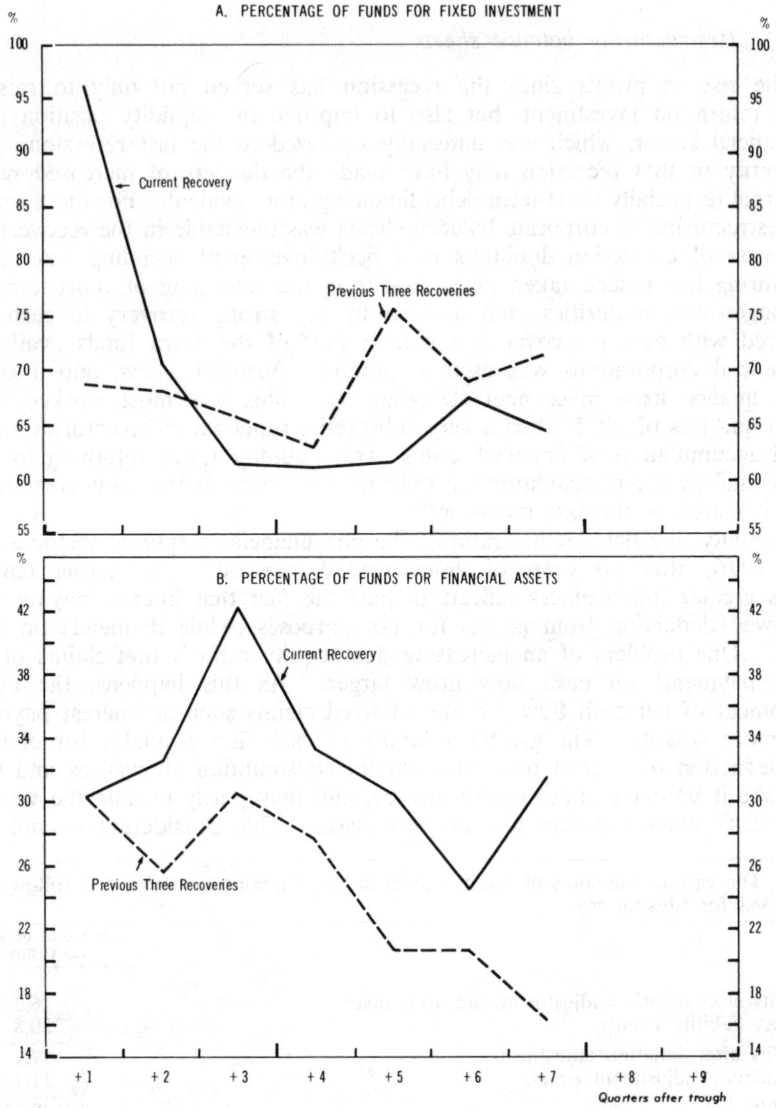

%   A. PERCENTAGE OF FUNDS FOR FIXED INVESTMENT   %

%   B. PERCENTAGE OF FUNDS FOR FINANCIAL ASSETS   %

                                                                          Quarters after trough

Source: Federal Reserve System, *Flow of Funds Accounts.*

importantly, perhaps, financial analysts' perception of it—undoubtedly contributed to the weakness of investment spending as firms were reluctant to increase external debt, and used much of the rising profits to rectify their debt/equity ratios[50].

50 The view that the debt/equity ratio has been allowed to rise too far appears to be quite widespread in the U.S. financial community. See Walter S. McConnell and Stephen D. Leit, "Inflation, Stock Prices and Job Creation", *Financial Analysts' Journal,* March/April, 1977.

Diagram 9 (Contd.) **Liquidity of non-financial corporations**

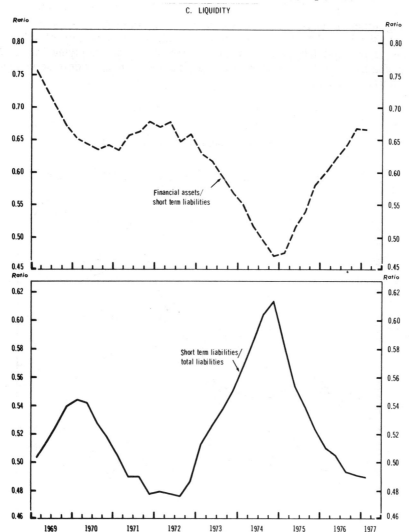

Source: Federal Reserve System, *Flow of Funds Accounts.*

(iii) *Cost of capital*

The cost of investment depends on the prices of the actual capital goods and on the costs of borrowing. The costs of capital investment have tended to rise faster than the prices of business sales, almost entirely because of the tendency for the increase in costs of buildings to exceed that of other components of GNP[51]. However, this has been a long-standing trend so that it is not clear

51 The fixed weight price index for business investment in structure in 1976 was up 65 per cent on 1970; that for investment in durable equipment was up by 45 per cent, very close to the 44 per cent rise for business GDP over the same period.

how it can explain the recent weakness in investment. Secondly, the price deflator
for non-residential investment has not risen significantly faster than labour costs[52],
providing little—if any—incentive for substituting labour for capital.   Thirdly,
there is in the United States some empirical evidence that the rate of substitution
between capital and labour is very low in the short run, implying that it takes
a large change in relative factor prices to induce even a modest adjustment in
the capital/labour ratio[53].

Diagram 10   Long-term rate of interest

1   Average yield on new issues of high-grade corporate bonds.
2   Nominal rate minus the change in the GNP deflator.
Source: Department of Commerce, *Survey of Current Business.*

52   Private non-farm business sector.
53   See: Nordhaus, W.D., "The Falling Share of Profits", *Brookings Papers on Economic
Activity,* 1974:1, pp. 169-219.

The nominal costs of long-term borrowing are still very high by historical standards, but this has not necessarily depressed investment since, on a simple definition, the "real" rate of interest[54] has been rather close to its long-run level (Diagram 10). The notion of "real" interest rates implies, though, that the current inflation rate is a good guide to expectations of *future* inflation: sharply decelerating inflation would naturally leave fixed-interest debtors saddled with high debt servicing charges. Finally, the alternative of raising funds on the stock market may have been dampened by continued investor wariness, which has kept price-earnings ratios for shares as a whole historically low[55].

(iv) Weaker expectations

Since investment decisions are heavily influenced by expectations about the future, the general weakness in business confidence has probably led to greater-than-usual caution in undertaking fixed investment. The absence—until very recently—of any measure of business confidence makes precise assessment impossible. Nonetheless, the continued low level of stock prices—by the end of 1976 they were still below the level of the 1970 recession quarter—is one striking indication of this caution. In part, this reflects a rather generalised scepticism—probably a product of the severity of the last recession—about the durability of the present recovery. With the disappearance of the post-war assurance that recessions would be only minor and short-lived affairs, firms have naturally become more cautious about their investment plans. This concern is exacerbated by the continuing high level of inflation. Though businessmen can adjust to, and plan for, a stable continuation of current inflation rates, the possibility of sharp changes in the rate of inflation inevitably adds to business uncertainty and gives rise to the fear that accelerating inflation could cause the Federal Reserve to pursue more restrictive policies and thus dampen growth and profit prospects. Finally, there is the additional uncertainty generated by changing legislation on pollution and on energy: this is probably particularly serious for the basic materials industries—where capacity shortages were so severe in 1973—which are typically both heavy polluters and large consumers of energy.

(v) Concluding remarks

From the above analysis it can be inferred that an important reason for the hitherto modest increases in investment has been the comparatively high degree of spare capacity in this recovery. Secondly, it is likely that investment has been depressed by the urgent need to restructure balance sheets after the ravages of the last (and, from the corporate viewpoint, unexpectedly severe) recession. This was especially true in 1975; however, this process by now seems to have run its course. Thirdly, it appears that the continued uncertainty—reflecting doubts about the sustainability of the recovery, fears of inflation, worries about the impact of prospective energy/pollution legislation—has adversely affected business spending. To what extent a possible deterioration in the cost/benefit balance of investment has depressed capital outlays is more difficult to say: though depending on measurement, profit rates can no longer be said to be severely depressed and the real long-term rate of interest is close to its normal level. On the other hand the cost of investing seems to have been rising faster than business

---

54 A conventional, though crude way of adjusting for inflation is to deflate the current rate of interest by changes in the GNP price deflator.

55 But this did not stop non-financial corporations from raising equity funds at the high annual rate of over $13 billion in the first half of 1976, but falling to only $6.2 billion in the second half of 1976.

Diagram 11 **Price index of shares (deflated)¹**
Trough quarter = 100

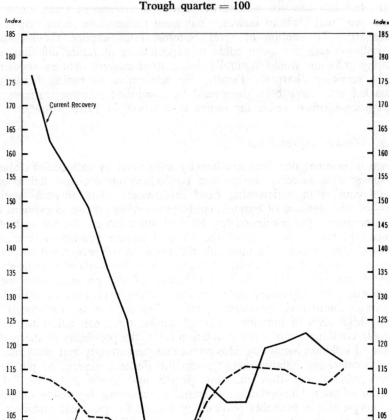

1   Standard and Poor's Combined Index of Common Stock Prices divided by the GNP deflator.

Source: Department of Commerce, *Survey of Current Business.*

sales prices in general, but it is unclear whether changes in relative factor prices have induced a shift in the desired capital/labour ratio.

The estimation of potential output

The developments described above led the outgoing Council of Economic Advisers to substantially revise the official estimates of potential GNP[56]. According

56   These revisions are described in the *Economic Report of the President*, 1977, pp. 52-56. The detailed work underlying the revision is described by Peter K. Clark, "A New Estimate of Potential GNP" (Council of Economic Advisers, unpublished, 1977).

to the old measure, actual GNP in 1976 was 11.0 per cent below potential, but the gap is now put at only 7.3 per cent. The main reason for the revision was a lower estimate of the underlying rate of productivity advance in the past: this explains about two-thirds of the revision. A second reason was that recent changes in the composition of the labour force—discussed above in the section "Labour market developments"—had raised the "full employment" unemployment rate from 4 per cent to 4.9 per cent by the mid-1970s. Finally, a measure of the capital stock was explicitly included, though this did not significantly affect the estimate of potential output[57].

In addition to revising the estimates of potential output in the past, the Council also estimated that potential GNP is in the near future likely to grow at an annual rate of 3½ per cent. Inevitably any estimate of the level as well as the growth of potential output is subject to a certain margin of error[58], and a more definitive picture will emerge only as the economy moves closer to the level of potential output. However, considering past trends and certain features of the 1970-1973 upturn, one issue would seem to be of particular relevance for near-term developments: the prospects for growth in the capital stock.

Table 8   **Capital, labour and capital/labour ratios**

	1954-1958	1958-1962	1962-1966	1966-1970	1970-1974	1975	1976
Growth rate of:							
Effective capital stock[1]	3.4	2.7	3.8	4.5	3.6	3.0	2.3
Full employment labour force	1.6	1.0	1.7	2.3	2.4	2.4	2.8
Potential capital/ labour ratio	1.8	1.7	2.1	2.2	1.2	0.6	−0.5

1   Fixed non-residential stock at 1972 prices, excluding pollution abatement capital.   Figures indicate average values of the capital stock per year.
Source: Council of Economic Advisers.

Prospects: capital investment and potential output

During the last couple of years, the combination of accelerating labour force growth and decelerating capital stock growth has led to virtual stagnation of the potential capital-labour ratio (Table 8). Consequently, capital utilisation rates in 1976 were associated with higher-than-usual unemployment rates, even adjusting for the changes in the composition of the labour force discussed above. Thus, the unemployment rate for married men was, in the second half of 1976, a full percentage point above the level in similar phases of earlier cycles[59]. This apparent shift raises the possibility that the capital stock will prove insufficient to fully employ the available labour force[60] so that it may be necessary to take

57   Peter K. Clark, op. cit. p. 10.
58   One recent alternative estimate, for example, puts the growth rate of potential output at 4.0 per cent and even higher [George L. Perry, "Potential Output and Productivity" (forthcoming)].
59   The unemployment rate for married men was 4.4 per cent in the second half of 1976, compared with the 3.5 per cent average for those quarters of earlier cycles with similar utilisation rates.
60   To the extent that some of the present job seekers are looking for part time jobs, the capital requirement will, of course, be correspondingly reduced.

explicit account of the capital stock in assessing future prospects for potential output and employment.

While the new estimates of potential output are influenced by such considerations, there is, nevertheless, a risk that the present degree of slack is smaller than suggested by the officially estimated GNP gap of 6-7 per cent[61]. Indeed, on the basis of past trends and the present outlook for business fixed investment (Part IV), a GNP growth at an average annual rate of 5 per cent might raise the rate of capacity utilisation in the industrial sector to around 88 per cent—which in 1973 was accompanied by supply bottlenecks in many industries and accelerating price increases—by the end of next year, while unemployment may not fall below 6-6¼ per cent[62]; i.e. stay 1½ percentage point above the unemployment rate underlying the official estimate of potential output.

Assessment of overall utilisation rates over the medium run is necessarily somewhat speculative at this stage. Thus, changes in the composition of demand in favour of services would reduce the rate of industrial production increase associated with a GNP growth of 5 per cent and a given expansion of industrial output may be associated with quite a broad range of changes in the capacity utilisation index, depending on the sectoral distribution of the overall increase[63]. Moreover, substitution of labour for capital, consequent on a possible change in relative factor prices and/or a demand shift towards labour intensive sectors, would also lower the aggregate capital/output ratio and hence postpone or prevent the emergence of capital shortage. On the other hand, in the event of substitution of labour for capital the rate of potential output growth is likely to fall below the officially estimated 3½ per cent, as the labour force would be spread more thinly over the available capital stock. This in turn would adversely affect the productivity performance, suggesting that a capital shortage may take the form of increased price and cost pressures rather than actual supply bottlenecks.

III ECONOMIC POLICY

With improved prospects for self-sustained recovery, demand management policies have shifted towards less stimulus since the autumn of 1975. The operation of automatic stabilisers and unintended spending shortfalls relative to initial budget appropriations have contributed to a sharp reduction in the public sector deficit. A further reduction of inflation has remained an important objective of monetary policy with the target ranges for money

---

61 In this context it is relevant to note that the revised estimates of potential GNP are based on the assumption that the extraordinary productivity decline during the recession is temporary. If, however, the shift in the level of productivity is more permanent, potential output may be 2-3 per cent lower than estimated. Cf. Peter Clark, op. cit. p. 27.

62 In 1972 Q1, the Federal Reserve's index of capacity utilisation in manufacturing stood at 80.9 per cent or close to the level recorded in the first quarter of this year. After seven quarters, an average expansion of GNP of 5 per cent (annual rate) per quarter—accompanied by an increase in industrial production of 7½ per cent—had increased the rate of capacity utilisation to near 88 per cent.

63 A characteristic feature of the 1973 situation was that supply bottlenecks developed at a rather early stage in the basic material industries, where physical production constraints are much more typical than in manufacturing. To what extent this development will be repeated in the present recovery is, of course, difficult to say, but it is important to note that investment spending in the basic material industries has been significantly higher than in manufacturing, and by April, 1977 the capacity margins in these industries were markedly higher than for the overall industrial sector.

supply growth being gradually lowered. However, given the continued above-trend rise in the velocity of circulation, the moderate growth of monetary aggregates has proved sufficient to accommodate the upswing at generally falling interest rates. In response to the recent re-acceleration of activity and stronger inflationary pressures, the Administration has withdrawn part of its earlier proposed package of fiscal stimulus and has announced new initiatives to curb cost and price increases.

FISCAL POLICY

The development of public sector revenue and expenditure during 1976 and into the first quarter of this year has exerted a dampening impact on the pace of the recovery:

(i) net taxes (total revenue less transfers to persons) advanced by 17 per cent between 1975 and 1976, outstripping the rate of growth of nominal incomes and raising the net average tax rate by almost 1 percentage point (Table 9);

(ii) public expenditure on goods and services increased by less than 8 per cent in current prices, significantly less than nominal GNP and corresponding to a real growth of only $1\frac{1}{4}$ per cent. As a result, the total public sector (including state and local governments) deficit (NIA basis), which in calendar year 1975 had reached almost $65 billion ($4\frac{1}{4}$ per cent of GNP), fell to less than $45 billion, with changes in the Federal Government deficit accounting for two-thirds of the decline.

While efforts to curb the rate of growth in public spending constituted an important element of restraint, and the non-recurrence of the 1975 tax rebate accounted for a large part of the increase in average tax rates, the main factor behind the shift in the overall thrust of budget policy was the influence of more or less automatic changes in revenue and expenditure. This was particularly so for Federal government transactions. Thus the Tax Reform Act of 1976 extended the provisions of the Revenue Adjustment Act of 1975[64], implying that effective tax rates were kept considerably below those incorporated in the 1974 tax law[65]. At the same time, the relatively slow growth in Federal spending on goods and services was strongly affected by an unintended shortfall in actual relative to projected expenditure. In the first three quarters of 1976 purchases of goods and services ran $2.8 billion below the projected rate, and during the same period transfer payments—including grants-in-aid—fell $3.8 billion short of the amounts envisaged in January, 1976. While the shortfall in personal transfers and grants-in-aid was to a large extent made up in the final quarter of 1976, expenditure on goods and services for the year as a whole was some $2 billion below previous predictions. Since the bulk of this shortfall occurred in the second quarter, it probably contributed to the unexpected "pause" in the recovery.

While the rise in state and local governments' receipts from own sources can be largely explained by the increased level of economic activity[66], expenditure patterns continued to reflect very cautious spending behaviour. For 1976 as a

---

64   The increases in the low income allowance and in the percentage standard deduction, introduced in 1975, were made permanent, while the personal tax credits and the reduction in corporate tax rates were extended to the end of 1977.

65   Compared with the 1974 legislation, the extension of the Revenue Adjustment Act meant a reduction in Federal taxes of $16 billion, while changes in the tax code incorporated in the Tax Reform Act of 1976 raised revenue by $600 million.

66   Only about 20 per cent of the increase in personal tax receipts was due to legislative actions and the introduction of a personal income tax in one state accounted for approximately half of this revenue increase.

Table 9   **Public sector revenue and expenditure**
National income accounts basis, calendar year

	1975 $ bill.	1974	1975	1976	1977[1]
			Per cent change		
Federal Government					
Personal taxes	125.7	14.5	−4.2	15.6	15
Corporate taxes	42.6	6.0	−6.6	31.2	9
Indirect taxes and social insurance contributions	118.2	10.8	6.0	9.4	12½
Total revenue	286.5	11.6	−0.6	15.4	13
Transfers, interest and subsidies	233.3	15.2	24.4	9.5	11
of which: Personal transfers	145.8	22.6	27.6	9.1	8½
Goods and services	124.4	9.2	11.5	7.2	10
Total expenditure	357.8	13.1	19.4	8.7	11
State and local government					
Personal taxes	43.1	8.6	9.9	12.1	10½
Corporate taxes	6.7	19.3	−1.5	31.3	10
Indirect taxes and social insurance contributions	130.1	8.4	8.1	10.1	8½
Grants-in-aid	54.4	8.1	23.9	10.7	18
Total revenue	234.3	8.6	11.5	11.2	11
Transfers, interest and subsidies	12.9	−13.1	14.2	10.1	5
Goods and services	214.5	14.5	12.0	8.3	7½
Total expenditure	227.4	12.5	12.1	8.4	7½
			$ billion		
Surplus before loan transactions		−4.2	−64.3	−44.6	−32.5
Federal government		−11.5	−71.2	−58.6	−58.0
State and local governments		7.3	6.9	14.0	25.5
			Per cent of GNP		
Memorandum items					
Surplus before loan transactions		−0.3	−4.2	−2.6	−1.7
Taxes less transfers[2]		21.4	18.4	19.1	19.5
Expenditure on goods and services		21.5	22.4	21.6	21.0

1 Secretariat forecast.
2 Excluding grants-in-aid and transfers to abroad.
Sources: Department of Commerce, *Survey of Current Business* and OECD Secretariat.

whole, expenditure on goods and services showed only a moderate advance of
1.3 per cent in real terms, compared with a long-term trend of 5-5½ per cent;
during the six months to March, 1977, local spending actually fell below that
of a year earlier. The weakening trend is partly a reflection of long-term
adjustments[67]. More important, however, has been the delay in reaction to the
1974-1975 recession and the related financial difficulties. As noted in last year's
Survey, the New York financial crisis adversely affected the market for municipal

67 Due to a declining school population, educational construction fell about 15 per cent,
and highway construction, probably due to a certain degree of saturation, fell 10 per cent.

bonds, and although the situation improved last year[68], attempts to bring expenditure into line with receipts seem to have continued. Thus, despite a marked deceleration in grants-in-aid payments[69], the surplus (NIA basis) rose considerably during 1976, reaching more than $20 billion by the first quarter of this year. Moreover, excluding the surplus on state and local government insurance funds, which are not available for financing capital spending or current deficits, the fiscal position (i.e. the operating balance) in the aggregate moved into surplus by the end of last year.

Adjusted for cyclically induced changes in revenue and expenditure, the improvement in the financial balance of the overall public sector was considerably smaller. Measured at the hypothetical income level corresponding to an overall unemployment rate of 4.9 per cent[70] the decline in the deficit between 1975 and 1976 was only $3½ billion compared with almost $13 billion for the actual balance (Diagram 12). While a declining "high employment" deficit would suggest a less expansionary policy stance, it should—as discussed in last year's Survey—be noted that some of the changes in this budget measure are of an automatic nature rather than the result of deliberate policy actions. Since the level of nominal income corresponding to an unemployment rate of 4.9 per cent gradually rises, and the income elasticity of tax revenues exceeds that of expenditure, the high employment deficit has a built-in tendency to decline over time. However, even if the decline in the "high employment" deficit exaggerates the degree of fiscal restraint in 1976, it is probably fair to say that discretionary fiscal measures had a slightly contractionary impact compared with the year before, when temporary measures played an important role.

MONETARY POLICY

A. *Money supply targets and monetary policy*

(a) *Background*

In formulating the broad policy approach for 1976-1977, the monetary authorities have continued to focus on a one-year time horizon for the growth of major monetary aggregates. The announcement of growth ranges for M_1, M_2 and M_3 was first made upon request from Congress in 1975 and they have been announced quarterly since[71]. This emphasis on the money stock as an indicator of monetary conditions reflects several interrelated developments:

(*i*) in the inflationary environment developing during the late 1960s and early 1970s, interest rates became more and more unreliable as an indicator of monetary conditions, as variations in nominal rates were increasingly dominated by inflationary expectations;

---

68 Rates in the municipal bond market have shown a general downward movement over the past 18 months and did not reverse course early this year, when other long-term rates increased.

69 The slow growth in grants-in-aid can probably to some extent be explained by a certain hesitancy in undertaking the matching and additional expenditure burden at the local level.

70 As noted in Part II, the outgoing Council of Economic Advisors' estimate of the "full employment rate of unemployment" was changed from 4 to 4.9 per cent, and the associated "high employment" deficit raised. The year-to-year changes in this budget measure are, however, only marginally affected by the revision.

71 In recent years, a number of other countries have also implemented monetary policy on the basis of projection of monetary aggregates, formulated in terms of ranges or a single point and based on one or more money supply measures.

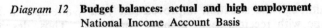

Diagram 12   Budget balances: actual and high employment
National Income Account Basis

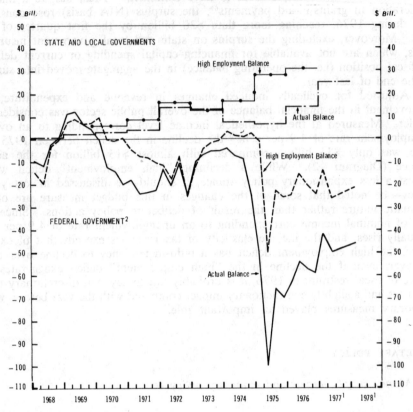

1   Secretariat forecast.
2   Seasonally adjusted, annual rate.
   Sources: Federal Reserve Bank of St. Louis, Council of Economic Advisers and OECD
Secretariat.

(ii)   at the same time it has become gradually recognised that if major
        disturbances to the economy originate in the real sector (rather than
        in the financial sector) a policy mainly framed in terms of the growth
        of monetary aggregates has a better chance of stabilising total income
        growth than a policy which attempts to prevent fluctuations in interest
        rates[72];

(iii) renewed interest in the role of money supply, as an important link
        between financial developments and the economy, has also influenced
        the new approach as the longer-run strategy explicitly aims at reducing
        money supply growth over time to rates compatible with long-run price
        stability.

72   If, for instance, the propensity to invest rises, a policy aimed at keeping the
growth of money supply constant and letting interest rates increase would tend to stabilise
total income growth. On the other hand, if the demand for money falls, a policy of keeping
interest rates constant by reducing the money supply increase would stabilise income growth.

(b) *Problems in setting and achieving growth ranges*

In determining money supply growth ranges consistent with both the long-range inflation target and the envisaged development of GNP over the projection period, the monetary authorities have faced several problems. Due to the highly inflationary environment characterising 1973-1974, and the persistence of inflationary expectations, a fast reduction of monetary growth to a non-inflationary level would inevitably have had serious consequences for the development of output and employment. The Federal Reserve System, therefore, adopted monetary growth ranges which it believed would neither brake the upswing nor re-accelerate inflation. However, as the rate of price and nominal income growth has tended to decline, the authorities have gradually reduced the growth ranges[73]. Thus, by early this year, the Federal Open Market Committee was operating with an upper boundary rate for M_1 that was a full percentage point lower than the rate postulated at the end of 1975, and the target ranges for the broader aggregate M_2 have also been adjusted downward, though the changes were less marked.

A second—and more technical—problem is that there does not exist a one-to-one relationship between nominal GNP and the money stock nor between the rate of growth of the various monetary aggregates for which targets are set. As noted below, changes in the public's desire to hold money balances in various forms can produce marked deviations from past patterns, implying in turn that a growth range for one aggregate may seem quite restrictive, while the targets for other aggregates may suggest an accommodating policy. Because of such slippages in the relationship between GNP and the money supply, there is a continued need for a close monitoring of interest rates and credit conditions as well as a need for a certain degree of flexibility in setting monetary growth ranges.

Apart from the problem of determining growth ranges consistent with GNP projections, the implementation of a policy based on stable growth in the supply of money is complicated by the fact that the money stock is endogenous (and therefore not subject to direct control). Moreover, short-term monetary movements tend to be of an erratic nature. Month-to-month and even quarter-to-quarter changes are highly volatile and attempts to even out such short-term variations could result in widely fluctuating interest rates. Partly as a consequence, the FOMC's instructions for the short-run conduct of monetary policy are given in terms of rather wide tolerance ranges for the bi-monthly growth rates in supply aggregates (Diagram 13) and geared to the control of the Federal Funds rate as the primary operative target[74].

(c) *Recent policy actions*

Over the last four quarters, M_1 has moved erratically around the lower end of the target range, attaining an average increase of $5\frac{1}{2}$ per cent. The growth of the broader aggregates M_2 and M_3 at respectively $10\frac{1}{2}$ and $12\frac{3}{4}$ per cent has generally been close to (or even above) the upper end of the range (Table 10). In view of the shifts between M_1 and time deposits included in M_2, the FOMC has more recently given increased weight to M_2 in its day-to-day operations. In general, the projected advance in monetary aggregates has been achieved with only moderate changes in money market conditions, as the Federal Funds

---

73 All but one of the ten changes in four-quarter growth ranges for M_1 and M_2, made over the past two years, have adjusted downward either the upper or the lower end of the ranges.

74 With the Federal Funds rate being used as an operative target, it can no longer serve as an indicator of monetary conditions, particularly since traders in the money market have become more reluctant to trade at rates perceived to be out of line with the System's objectives.

Diagram 13   Short-term tolerance ranges for monetary variables

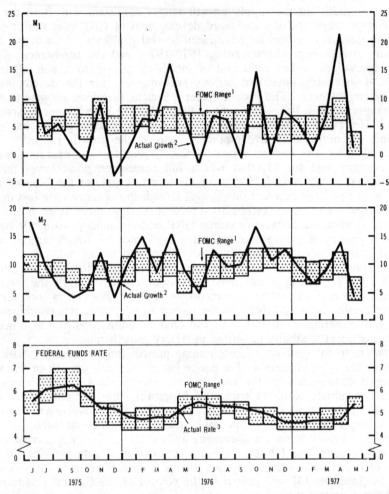

1   The tolerance ranges result from monthly meetings of the Federal Open Market Committee (FOMC) and are specified in relation to the month of the meeting and the following month.
2   Annual rate of change during month.
3   Monthly averages of daily figures.
Source: Federal Reserve System, Federal Reserve Bulletin.

rate—the interest rate of interbank loans of immediately available funds on an overnight basis—has varied between 4¾ and 5½ per cent for most of the period:

(i)   early in the second quarter of 1976, when expectations of a continued strong economic expansion were widespread and Treasury transactions spurred the growth of monetary aggregates, a somewhat tighter stance was adopted, and the Federal Funds rate rose to about 5½ per cent in late May. However, when the growth of the aggregates returned to rates within the long-term ranges, steps were taken to provide bank reserves more freely;

Table 10 **Monetary projections and actual growth of major monetary aggregates 1975/1977**
Per cent change from a year earlier

Period	M₁	M₂	M₃
March 1976			
Projected range	5-7½	8½-10½	10-12
Actual	4.9	9.6	12.2
1976 Q2			
Projected range	5-7½	8½-10½	10-12
Actual	5.2	9.6	12.0
1976 Q3			
Projected range	5-7½	7½-10½	9-12
Actual	4.4	9.3	11.5
1976 Q4			
Projected range	4½-7½	7½-10½	9-12
Actual	5.4	10.5	12.3
1977 Q1			
Projected range	4½-7	7½-10	9-12
Actual	6.0	10.6	12.6
Projections			
1977 Q2	4½-7	7½-9½	9-11
1977 Q3	4½-6½	7½-10	9-11½
1977 Q4	4½-6½	7-10	8½-11½
1978 Q1	4½-6½	7-9½	8½-11

NOTE M₁ is currency plus demand deposits; M₂ is M₁ plus time deposits at commercial banks other than large negotiable certificates of deposits; and M₃ is M₂ plus deposits at non-bank thrift institutions.
Source: Board of Governors of the Federal Reserve System.

(*ii*)   in the second half of 1976, as the slower pace of economic activity reduced the demand for credit as well as the rate of growth of monetary supply, the Federal Reserve fostered further easing of market rates, and the Federal Funds rate declined to 4 5/8 per cent by the end of the year[75];

(*iii*) when developments in early 1977 re-ignited inflationary expectations, causing a marked rise in medium and long-term interest rates, the authorities kept the Federal Funds rate constant, but during the early spring, following a sharp acceleration in the growth of monetary aggregates, open market operations became more restrictive, and the Federal Funds rate edged towards the 5 3/8 per cent level by the end of May.

B.   *Monetary and financial developments*

The unusually low growth of M₁ relative to GNP as well as other monetary aggregates, which had characterised the early phase of the recovery, continued

75   In addition, complementary adjustments were made in other instruments of monetary policy. The discount rate was cut by ¼ percentage point to 5¼ per cent (22nd November, 1976), and a modest cut in reserve requirement on time deposits with effect from early January, 1977 was announced in December.

Diagram 14 **Interest rates and changes in velocity of M₁**

A. SELECTED INTEREST RATES

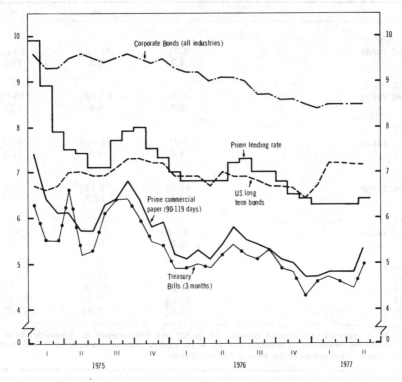

Source: Federal Reserve System, *Federal Reserve Bulletin.*

through 1976 and into this year. Contrary to most predictions made a year ago, the rise in M₁ has remained low in spite of a brisk pick-up in nominal income and declining levels of interest rates, normally expected to act as a drag on velocity. This increasing desire of the general public to economise on their M₁ balances can be attributed to several factors (already explored in last year's Survey[76]), notably a growing availability of interest-bearing alternatives for transaction purposes. Another important element may have been a decline in business holdings of compensating balances, induced by the shift in the structure of financing from a heavy reliance on bank loans to open market instruments, and from short-term to long-term borrowing[77]. Finally, the declining level of money market rates has created interest differentials in favour of interest-bearing deposits as an outlet for shorter-term financial investment, thus boosting the growth of M₂ and M₃.

---

76   As can be seen from Diagram 14, velocity growth generally moves quite erratically in the short run. However, a three quarters moving average displays a clear pro-cyclical behaviour and a marked acceleration in the early phase of the current recovery.

77   The weak growth in bank lending was mainly the result of sluggish investment demand but may have been influenced by the interest rate policy of commercial banks. Thus, the differential between banks' prime lending rate and the rate on commercial paper increased by almost one percentage point from mid-1975 to end-1976.

Diagram 14 (Contd.) **Interest rates and changes in velocity of M₁**

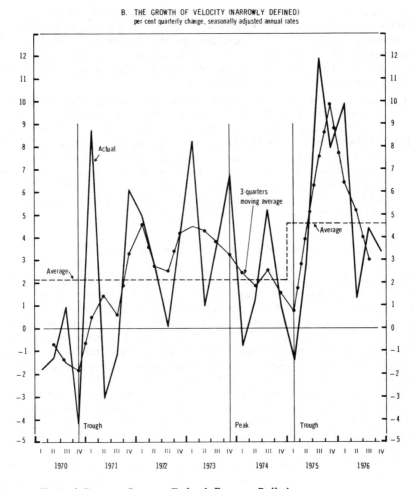

B. THE GROWTH OF VELOCITY (NARROWLY DEFINED)
per cent quarterly change, seasonally adjusted annual rates

Source: Federal Reserve System, *Federal Reserve Bulletin.*

Contrary to widely-held expectations, interest rates declined throughout most of 1976, in some cases to the lowest levels for three years[78]. Both long and short-term rates were rising quite sharply early in 1976 as market participants—anticipating growing competition between rapidly expanding private credit demand and heavy public sector borrowing—over-reacted to the moderate tightening of money market conditions. However, this trend was reversed in the second half as the pace of the economic expansion slowed considerably and the Federal deficit as well as business demand for credit fell short of expectations. In early 1977 most interest rates rose as anticipations of a further decline in the Federal

---

78   During the first 18 months of three of the five previous post-war recoveries, interest rates increased; the decline registered in 1971 may be attributed to a sudden fall in inflationary expectations, following the announcement of the wage-price freeze.

Funds rate proved to be wrong, while clear signs of a stronger-than-expected underlying growth trend, fears of an excessive Federal deficit, and an acceleration of prices adversely affected the medium-term outlook for inflation[79].

The general fall in the level of interest rates during 1976 was accompanied by a slight steepening of the yield curve, which became temporarily somewhat more pronounced in early 1977. On average, declines in the shorter end of the market attained 75 to 100 basis points, while reductions in the longer end were 25 to 50 points. The general stickiness of long-term interest rates may be related to continued high inflation rate expectations:

(i)   although the Federal budget deficit was smaller than expected, the Treasury raised $62 billion—second only to the record amount raised in 1975—mainly by selling intermediate-term coupon securities;

(ii) as discussed in Part II, the non-financial corporate sector continued to build up liquid reserves and to lengthen the maturity structure of debts. Attempting to secure long-term funds before the expected rise in interest rates, corporate firms virtually flooded the bond market during the first half of 1976, with the proceeds being used for retiring short-term debt or for investing in short-term assets.

C.   Developments in financial balances and demand for credit

The unusually large swings in domestic financial balances, which had characterised the early phase of the current recovery, were partially reversed in the course of 1976. Influenced by the fall in the household savings rate as well as the strong pick-up in residential investment, the saving surplus of the private sector was cut in half between 1975 and 1976 (Table 11), with the change being mirrored in a smaller public sector deficit and a deterioration in the current external balance. In line with the decline in net private saving, the credit demand of the private sector rose by almost 55 per cent from 1975 to 1976, of which more than half was accounted for by households; corporate borrowing, though increasing, remained almost 30 per cent below the earlier peak level.

Although the public sector deficit fell sharply—and more than anticipated—the financing of the deficit continued to dominate credit market developments. Thus, in the second half of 1976, when the deficit had declined to around $40 billion, borrowing by the U.S. Government accounted for almost 25 per cent of total funds raised, compared with less than 9 per cent on average during the 1970-1974 period. Moreover, while the 30 per cent decline in private credit demand had "made room" for the financing of the public deficit in 1975, the budget imbalance for 1976 had to be accommodated during a period when private sector demands were beginning to increase. Finally, changes in the structure of interest rates induced substantial reintermediation[80].

Nevertheless, the financing of the Federal deficit was accommodated rather smoothly. Interest rates were generally falling during 1976[81] and the Treasury was able to extend the average maturity of the public debt:

---

79   Rates of three-month Treasury bills increased from 4.35 per cent in December to 4.60 in March, and the yield on five-year government securities rose from 6.10 to 6.93 per cent during the same period.

80   Since rates on time and saving deposits are changed rather infrequently, the decline in Treasury bill rates during 1976 created interest rate differentials in favour of commercial and savings bank deposits.

81   It may, of course, be argued that in the absence of the large public sector deficit, long-term interest rates would have declined considerably more and that in this sense public sector transactions led to some "crowding out". On the other hand, less fiscal support to private income would certainly have had a dampening impact on investment.

Table 11 **Financial balances**

	1973	1974	1975	1976	1975[5] H. 1	1975[5] H. 2	1976[5] H. 1	1976[5] H. 2
					$ Billion			
A Domestic saving-investment balances[1]								
Private	−9.5	−5.4	71.9	35.2	76.7	67.1	42.1	28.3
Public	6.3	−4.2	−64.4	−44.6	−69.0	−59.8	−48.3	−41.0
B Funds raised in US credit market by non-financial sectors	197.6	188.8	210.4	257.7	184.2	236.5	238.3	277.2
US Government	8.3	12.0	85.2	68.9	80.8	89.6	71.7	66.2
Other domestic non-financial sectors	183.1	161.6	112.2	168.5	94.9	129.4	151.1	185.8
Households	73.5	45.2	49.7	80.2	39.0	60.4	71.9	88.5
Corporate sector	72.9	83.1	37.1	53.1	33.5	40.6	47.3	58.8
State and local governments	14.8	18.6	14.9	17.7	13.9	15.9	16.2	19.3
Other domestic sectors	22.0	14.6	10.6	17.4	8.6	12.6	15.7	19.2
Foreign sector	6.2	15.3	13.0	20.3	8.5	17.4	15.4	25.2
					Share in per cent			
C Federal debt issue by purchasing sector[2]								
FR Banks	108.9	17.9	8.6	13.1	11.5	6.5	19.4	7.3
Commercial banks	−93.7	−42.0	34.4	25.1	37.4	33.6	20.0	29.9
Other financial sectors[3]	−8.9	−6.3	6.1	5.8	5.5	6.5	5.4	6.1
Households	41.8	68.8	7.5	13.7	6.0	7.7	15.2	12.3
Non-financial firms	13.9	0.9	10.7	7.6	6.0	14.2	14.3	1.4
Foreign and international	3.8	25.9	9.5	16.7	20.9	1.0	9.9	23.2
Others[4]	34.2	34.8	23.3	17.9	12.6	30.6	15.8	19.8

1 NIA basis.
2 Excluding purchases by US Government Agencies and Trust Funds.
3 Mutual savings banks and insurance companies.
4 Including state and local governments.
5 Seasonally adjusted annual rates.
Sources: Federal Reserve System, *Federal Reserve Bulletin* and Economic Report of the President 1977.

(*i*) more flexible and efficient marketing procedures[82] together with the offering of a wider range of maturities enabled the authorities to sell large quantities of public securities without raising the level of interest rates;

(*ii*) the marked improvement in the financial position of the corporate sector was to a large extent reflected in higher demand for Treasury bills; at the same time, continued low corporate demand for loans induced banks to increase their holdings of medium and longer-term government papers;

82 Several measures were introduced to improve the market's reception of the debt issues: (*i*) estimates of financing needs were made public, (*ii*) offerings of coupon issues were regularized to an even greater extent than in 1975, and (*iii*) fixed price issues were offered on three occasions when market conditions were favorable to direct placement of securities with ultimate investors. In addition, the Congress increased the amount of government bonds exempt from interest ceiling and increased the maximum maturity of notes from seven years to ten years.

(*iii*)   while households reduced their stock of Treasury bills, they invested
heavily in savings bonds and other long-term securities and the marked
rise in time and savings deposit inflows enabled savings banks to place
excess reserves in long- and medium-term securities.

POLICIES UNDERLYING THE 1977-1978 OUTLOOK

(a)   *Demand management policy*

Recently voted amendments to the FY 1977 budget[83] together with the
First Concurrent Resolution for next year's budget make fiscal policy more expansionary during the forecast period (to mid-1978), with most of the stimulus coming
in the next 2-3 quarters:

(*i*)   higher standard deductions for personal income taxes have been introduced as from 1st June with retroactive effect from the beginning of
1977, entailing a reduction in revenues of $5½ billion at an annual
rate;

(*ii*)   an employment tax credit will be granted as from 1st July, with the
reduction in corporate taxes estimated at $2½ billion on a full year
basis;

(*iii*)   new public work programmes, increases in public service jobs and
training programmes, and counter-cyclical grants to state and local
governments will raise Federal expenditure by almost $12 billion over
the forecast period, with the bulk of the increase falling in FY 1978.

Together with extensions (until the end of 1978) of the temporary tax
reductions incorporated in the Tax Reform Act of 1976, the revenue measures
should keep the rate of growth of Federal taxes over the next five quarters
well below previous rates, with the average Federal tax burden likely to show a
small decline between the first and the second half of this year. Assuming no
major spending shortfalls, Federal purchases of goods and services (real terms)
and intergovernmental transfers should accelerate strongly over the next couple
of quarters as the employment measures take effect. Thereafter expenditure trends
are likely to weaken as the recommended ceiling on Federal spending incorporated in the First Concurrent Resolution implies a decline in the rate of growth in
total outlays (current prices) between fiscal 1977 and 1978. As a result of the
recently adopted policy measures, the budget deficit (NIA basis) can be expected
to rise in the early part of FY 1978, but anticipating some fall in the course
of the year, the authorities are forecasting a largely unchanged Federal deficit
for the next fiscal year as a whole. Reflecting the discretionary actions taken,
the "high employment" deficit is also likely to rise over the near term.

On the other hand, the budget surplus of state and local governments may
increase substantially. Given the long lags with which increases in inter-govern-
mental transfers affect local spending, and the recent hesitant spending behaviour
of local governments, the projected large increases in Federal counter-cyclical
grants and other grants-in-aid payments (Table 9) cannot be expected to result
in additional purchases much before the end of this year. Moreover, the sluggish
employment growth over the last two years points to a high degree of substitution
between new Federally funded jobs and existing jobs in the state and local

_____

83   As noted above, a package of stimulative measures totalling $31 billion for FY 1977
and 1978 was proposed in February (for details, see Annex II). Subsequent changes reduced
the size of the package, notably for 1977 and the revised version together with other budgetary
changes was adopted by Congress in the Third Concurrent Resolution.

sector[84]. The re-establishment of a surplus on the operating account for the aggregate state and local government sector has removed an important constraint on their budgetary actions. Consequently, state and local authorities may increase expenditure and/or reduce their own-source revenues, but given the likely rise in the budget surplus of these authorities, the overall economic impact of their transactions may nevertheless be restrictive, thus partly offsetting the effect of Federal operations.

As noted, the exceptionally strong growth of monetary aggregates in April prompted the authorities to adopt a more restrictive policy stance, with the Federal Funds rate permitted to rise above 5 per cent. Moreover, the money supply target ranges announced for the year ending in the first quarter of 1978[85], in conjunction with the Secretariat forecast for nominal GNP (Part IV) imply a further rise of $6\frac{1}{2}$ per cent in the income velocity of M_1, compared with a 4 per cent increase over the previous four quarters. In earlier cyclical upturns the rate of growth in velocity has typically fallen despite rising interest rates. Nevertheless, the present stance of monetary policy—even allowing for a substantially higher public sector credit demand than in corresponding phases of earlier cycles—would on balance seem to be consistent with a relatively moderate rise in interest rates. Hence the Secretariat forecast is based on the assumption that short-term rates may rise by no more than 1-$1\frac{1}{2}$ percentage point over the forecast period and long-term rates rather less, entailing some narrowing of the yield spread, a typical feature of previous upturns.

In addition to a likely further downward shift in the demand for M_1[86], the outlook for real and financial developments in the private sector suggests that private credit demand will remain weak relative to the overall level of activity, thus restraining the upward movement of interest rates:

(i)   the predicted pick-up in business fixed investment and inventory formation (see below) will probably lead to a rise in business credit demand, but the marked improvement in the financial position of the corporate sector and the still relatively subdued level of investment suggest that loan demand will remain low by the standards of previous recoveries;

(ii) the forecast strong rise in residential investment and a likely sharp increase in construction costs[87] are bound to push up demand for mortgage loans; however, the exceptionally large deposit inflows to thrift institutions during 1976 and their likely continuation over most of the forecast period should ensure an adequate supply of mortgage funds at roughly stable or moderately rising interest rates;

(iii) given the general improvement in sectoral balance sheets and some likely increase in the personal savings rate, the forecast upswing in GNP should to a larger degree than in previous cyclical recoveries

---

84   In 1976, despite the increased availability of Federal grants, employment in the state and local government sector increased by 2 per cent, compared with $5\frac{1}{2}$ per cent on average during the preceding 10 years.

85   For the year ending in the first quarter of 1978, the official target ranges of growth are $4\frac{1}{2}$-$6\frac{1}{2}$ per cent for M_1, 7-$9\frac{1}{2}$ per cent for M_2, and $8\frac{1}{2}$ and 11 per cent for M_3.

86   As noted earlier, the demand for M_1 has tended to shift down in recent years, allowing interest rates to fall despite an above-trend increase in the velocity of M_1. Some of the institutional changes contributing to this development should continue to moderate the rate of growth of M_1 during the forecast period. At the same time, the forecast development in interest rates suggests that the rate of growth of the broadly-defined money supply M_2 will slow down relative to that of M_1, as the general rise in interest rates will probably be accompanied by a reversal of the present yield differential in favour of time and saving deposits.

87   By the first quarter of this year the implicit deflator for residential construction was $6\frac{3}{4}$ per cent above the average for 1976.

be "financed" by internal funds, with available liquid assets serving to prevent interest rates from rising too sharply.

(b) Other policy developments

In April the Administration announced a long list of measures designed to bring the rate of inflation down to the 4-4½ per cent range by the end of 1979. Later in the month a National Energy Plan was proposed, aiming at reducing the annual rate of growth of energy consumption to 2 per cent by 1985 (4½ per cent in 1976) and encouraging domestic production of alternative energy sources, notably coal[88]. While the anti-inflation programme will take effect during 1977-1978, the type of measures announced[89] makes it difficult to quantify the impact on price and wage developments. The National Energy Plan, if enacted by Congress in its present form, would directly affect price and output developments in the first half of 1978. However, due to uncertainties about the timing of legislative actions, the forecast presented below does not allow for any specific influence of the programme during the period under consideration. It should be noted, though, that even if the proposed measures do not become effective before 1978, anticipatory effects could well have some influence on the strength and pattern of final domestic demand already in 1977.

IV SHORT-TERM PROSPECTS

As noted earlier, the pace of economic activity has picked up considerably in recent months, fuelled largely by exceptionally large gains in consumer spending and residential construction. Forward-looking indicators (Diagram 15) point to continued strong increases in demand and output in the next few months, though the spectacular gains in March/April may partly reflect catch-up effects following the cold weather earlier in the year. Looking further ahead, prospects for strong growth through the first half of 1978 are generally viewed as favourable, with quarterly increases in GNP predicted to be in the 5 to 5½ per cent range (Table 12)[90]. The following paragraphs discuss in more detail the outlook for different demand components, employment, prices and wages, and the external balance[91].

Outlook for demand, output and employment

Current evidence suggests continued strong gains in all major components of final demand. The recent buoyancy of housing starts and building permits implies further sharp growth in residential investment during the second quarter and possibly beyond[92]. With vacancy rates declining and ample availability of mortgage funds, the construction of rental units—so far a laggard in the

---

88   Details of the two programmes are given in Annex II.

89   The anti-inflation programme mainly relies on structural improvements, consultations with labour and management, and a review of the cost effect and efficiency of various government regulations.

90   The most recent (May, 1977) forecasts published by the Wharton School of Economics and Data Resources imply average quarterly increases of respectively 6½ and 5½ per cent for the period until the second quarter of 1978.

91   For the main policy assumptions underlying the Secretariat forecast, see Part III.

92   Housing starts and number of building permits in March reached the highest levels for almost four years.

Table 12 **OECD forecasts**

Seasonally adjusted per cent changes at annual rates, 1972 prices

	1975	1976	1977	1975 II	1976 I	1976 II	1977 I	1977 II	1978 I
Demand and output									
Private consumption	1.5	5.6	5.2	4.9	6.5	4.5	6.2	3.8	3.9
Total government purchases	1.8	1.2	1.0	4.5	−0.8	2.0	−1.8	5.6	6.5
Non-residential investment	−13.3	3.9	10.0	−3.9	6.4	7.1	11.2	10.4	11.3
Residential investment	−14.7	22.5	16.6	27.4	21.4	20.3	16.5	13.4	7.4
Gross fixed capital formation	−13.7	8.7	11.9	3.3	10.3	10.7	12.7	11.3	10.1
Final domestic demand	−0.7	5.0	5.2	4.6	5.4	4.8	5.4	5.2	5.3
Inventory change[1]	−1.7	1.7	0.4	3.0	2.3	−0.8	0.8	0.6	0.1
Total domestic demand	−2.4	6.8	5.5	7.9	7.8	3.9	6.2	5.8	5.4
Exports	−6.7	6.0	4.9	7.6	4.8	6.9	2.6	7.7	6.9
Imports	−15.7	17.7	10.1	7.8	27.2	10.1	9.6	11.0	9.6
Net exports[1]	0.5	−0.6	−0.3	0.1	−1.1	−0.1	−0.4	−0.1	−0.1
GNP	−1.8	6.1	5.2	7.9	6.5	3.7	5.7	5.6	5.2
GNP deflator	9.3	5.1	5.7	6.4	4.5	5.0	5.9	6.1	6.3

1 Change on an annual basis as a per cent of GNP of previous period.

Sources: Department of Commerce, Survey of Current Business and OECD Secretariat.

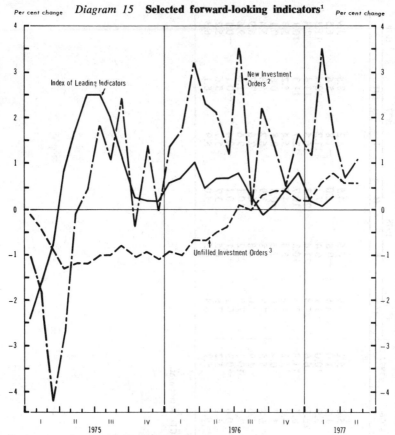

Per cent change   *Diagram 15*   **Selected forward-looking indicators**[1]   Per cent change

1   Percentage changes of three-month moving averages.
2   Net new orders, non-defence capital goods (current prices).
3   Unfilled orders, non-defence capital goods (current prices).

Source: Department of Commerce, *Business Conditions Digest* and *Survey of Current Business.*

recovery—can be expected to accelerate, while investment in single-family units may flatten out. On balance, some slowdown in the overall rate of growth appears probable as total housing starts are now approaching historical peak levels (Diagram 16). Moreover, the envisaged strengthening of business demand for loans may bid funds away from the mortgage sector and/or raise long-term interest rates, though financial developments are unlikely to constrain residential construction much before well into next year.

Some uncertainty continues to surround the prospects for business fixed investment. During the last four quarters, real non-residential capital spending has been growing at an average annual rate of over $8\frac{1}{2}$ per cent. Forward-looking indicators[93] and some private survey results[94] suggest even greater buoyancy for

93   In the first quarter of 1977, new orders (current prices) for non-defence capital goods were 13 per cent above the 1976 average level.
94   According to a Conference Board survey, capital appropriations (current prices) of manufacturing industries in the fourth quarter of 1976 exceeded the average level of the first three quarters of 1976 by 30 per cent and this rise was maintained in the first quarter of this year. Moreover, a recent survey by McGraw-Hill Publications suggests that business fixed investment may increase by as much as 11 per cent (real terms) in 1977.

Diagram 16 **Housing starts**[1]
Seasonally adjusted

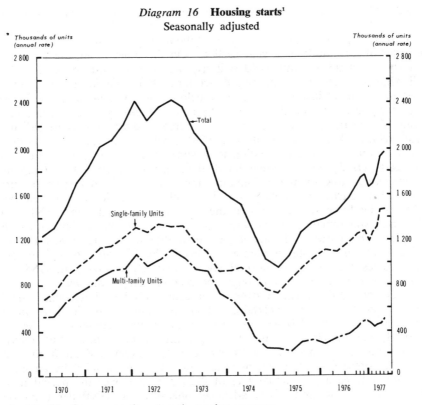

1 Monthly figures are three-month moving averages.
Source: Department of Commerce, *Business Conditions Digest.*

1977. And by May capacity utilisation in manufacturing was only $4\frac{1}{2}$ percentage points below the 1973 peak, suggesting that a strong increase in capital spending may be about to materialise. On the other hand, there are indications that the rate of capacity utilisation needed to spark off a strong recovery of business fixed investment has been rising during recent cyclical upturns. In addition, the most recent official investment survey presents a somewhat weaker picture, pointing to a $7\frac{1}{2}$ per cent increase between 1976 and 1977 and a considerable deceleration from the first to the second half of this year. Taking account, however, of the recent strength of the economic recovery and assuming that—in line with previous cyclical upturns—actual spending will exceed anticipated levels of capital outlays, the most likely development of business fixed investments would seem to be a continuation of last year's pace during 1977, with a slight acceleration in the first half of 1978 as capacity utilisation rates increase.

Private consumption, although probably losing some strength, should nevertheless remain a mainstay of the upswing[95]. Average tax rates are predicted to rise less in 1977 than in 1976, and on the basis of current and prospective output and productivity trends (see below) further strong employment gains can be

95 The financial position of households has remained strong. The ratio of financial assets to financial liabilities was still higher by the fourth quarter of 1976 than it was in 1974 and 1975, despite a marked rise in consumer credit in the second half of last year.

expected. Other household income components are generally foreseen to show a continued fast advance. Thus, despite an acceleration in consumer prices, the gain in real disposable income in 1977 (about 4 per cent) should be of the same order of magnitude as a year earlier. On the other hand, the savings rate is unlikely to fall further and could well rise over the forecast period[96].

Taking account of the envisaged acceleration in public spending and the forecast development in foreign trade (see below) total final sales can be expected to rise at an average annual rate of 5-5¼ per cent through the forecast period. The rate of growth of GNP over the next couple of quarters may be still higher as firms rebuild their lean inventories. The stocks/final sales ratios early this year fell to very low levels, pointing to a substantial rise in stockbuilding over the forecast period. On the other hand, if firms remain cautious, attempting to keep inventories low or underestimating the strength of final sales, a further decline—albeit partly involuntary—in the stock/sales ratios could well occur. The Secretariat forecast assumes that the inventory/final sales ratio (NIA basis, 1972 prices) will remain roughly stable at the low first quarter level throughout the coming 5-6 quarters. It should be noted that the output forecast is quite sensitive to changes in this assumption; indeed, should firms attempt to restore inventory/sales ratio to more normal levels, quarterly advances in GNP could average more than 7 per cent through the second half of the year.

A rate of GNP growth of over 5 per cent should lead to some reduction of unemployment, though uncertainty about the rate of productivity increase and the growth of the labour force clouds the picture somewhat. As noted in Part II, the labour force has been growing rapidly during this recovery, although with some slowdown occurring recently. Assuming no further trend change, the forecast development in output may be accompanied by an increase in the labour force at an annual rate of 2-2½ per cent over the period to mid-1978[97]. The rate of productivity advance—measured as GNP per employee—can be expected to strengthen during the first half of this year—partly because of a likely increase in average hours worked—but may well slacken thereafter, though probably remaining above the long-term trend. On this basis, and taking account of the employment measures to be introduced during the second half of this year, the rate of unemployment could well fall to around 6½ per cent by mid-1978.

Prices and wages

Recent price movements have been characterised by a relatively steady advance of wholesale prices of industrial commodities but sharp increases for food and some basic materials which pushed the annual rate of the overall price index to over 8½ per cent in the first quarter of this year. Much of this acceleration reflects a one-time and possibly reversible effect of the severe winter on food and fuel prices. In fact, following a rise of more than 10 per cent during the first three months of this year, food commodities' prices have flattened since early April and actually declined in May.

Though it cannot be excluded that the recent acceleration of prices—however temporary—could ignite inflationary expectations and entail higher wage claims,

---

96 Influenced by the sharp rise in fuel and food prices, the savings rate in the first quarter of this year was probably unsustainably low, as heating and food normally have very low price elasticities. It is also possible that the announcement of the $50 tax rebate had an expansionary impact on household spending, notably on durable goods. Another special factor was the large gift tax payments in the first quarter as a result of changes in the tax law.

97 Despite the recent slowdown in the rate of growth, the labour force in April exceeded the previous year's level by almost 3 per cent.

present indications on collective bargaining settlements do not point to such a development[98]. Even so, some short-lived acceleration in the advance of hourly earnings would seem likely since approximately 50 per cent of existing wage contracts contain provisions for cost-of-living adjustments. However, with labour market conditions remaining rather weak, and good prospects for some deceleration in food and fuel prices, a certain moderation of wage increases should take place during the second half of the year, notwithstanding the fact that 1977 is a heavy bargaining year. On these assumptions, the rise in average compensation per employee is unlikely to exceed $8\frac{1}{2}$ per cent between 1976 and 1977 and may show a similar trend rise into 1978. Together with the expected decline in the rate of labour productivity growth, this suggests that prospects for a slowdown of unit labour cost increases below an annual rate of 6 per cent are not very favourable in the near future. On the other hand, profit margins may not show any further significant rise, so that the overall rate of inflation, as measured by the implicit GNP deflator, may also be kept within the 6 per cent range. However, given the larger weight of food products, the rise in consumer prices could well come close to 7 per cent, but, disregarding the proposed energy programme, should decelerate early next year.

The current external balance

Since the United States continues to lead the world recovery, the trade balance is expected to move further into deficit, though not as rapidly as of late since much of the recent deterioration probably reflects temporary factors, particularly the high level of fuel demand. Thus the volume of imports is likely to decline in the second quarter, but influenced by the forecast strong inventory formation, a relatively high rate of growth of industrial production, and some shift in private consumption towards purchases of durable goods, the increase in the volume of imports over the remainder of the forecast period may average close to 10 per cent (annual rate). The share of oil in total merchandise imports can be expected to fall, particularly towards the end of the year when Alaskan oil production is coming on stream.

Agricultural exports, after bulging to a $24\frac{1}{2}$ billion annual rate in the second half of last year, are expected to hold roughly steady in first half 1977 (with stronger prices substantially offsetting a distinct volume decline) before sliding off to annual rates of something less than $24 billion in the second half and the first half 1978. Non-agricultural export volume, after declining slightly in both the last quarter 1976 and the first quarter this year, is predicted to rise at a 4-5 per cent annual rate over most of the forecast period as a continued sluggish export growth to non-oil LDCs is expected to offset a marked improvement of export markets in major industrial countries. All in all, the outlook in real terms would suggest a further increase of last year's trade deficit, with a likely terms-of-trade deterioration bringing the prospective deficit to about $25 billion in 1977 (BoP basis). With the invisible surplus probably improving by a further $2 billion, the current account may show a deficit of somewhere around $14 billion, after virtual balance in 1976. No major change is foreseen for the first half of 1978.

---

98 Major collective bargaining settlements reached during the first quarter generally provided for smaller first year increases than 1976 agreements, and annual wage rate adjustments over the life of the contract were only slightly larger than those for 1976. On the other hand, hourly compensations (private business) in the first quarter accelerated to an annual rate of almost 11 per cent.

V   CONCLUSIONS

The economic outlook has considerably improved over the last six months, partly due to a spontaneous strengthening of demand but also as a result of new policy measures.   With the policies now in place, a satisfactory rate of growth over the coming 12 months, with a fall in unemployment, seems secured; if anything, the expansion could be rather stronger than envisaged, particularly over the next two quarters, due to stronger stockbuilding.   As far as one can judge at present, no major change in the general stance of demand management policy should be necessary in the near future.   But additional selective action would seem desirable, particularly in two areas:

(a) unemployment is very high among young people and adult women. Recorded unemployment for those under 25 years has risen significantly over the last few years to a rate of around 13 per cent.   The rate for women (6.6 per cent) is also well above the average for male adults. Experience from both the United States and other countries suggests that selective policies can have important effects in individual segments of the labour market without adding much to aggregate demand;

(b) since the late 1960s the rapid trend growth of the labour force— accompanied by a shift in its composition towards less efficient labour— together with a virtually stagnant stock of productive capital has entailed slower productivity growth.   It may also have meant that a certain imbalance has developed in the sense that, even at full capacity operation, the existing capital stock may not be sufficient to employ all those able and willing to work.   A strong increase in investment will therefore be needed to correct this imbalance and, in view of recent cyclical experience, it cannot be taken for granted that this will develop spontaneously.   Since a given rate of growth in total output may be associated with a wide range of investment requirements, depending on the composition of output and possible changes in the capital/labour ratio, any assessment of a potential capital shortage is extremely hazardous.   Nevertheless, on the present outlook for business fixed investment it cannot be excluded that the economy may absorb existing capacity margins before new projects come on stream, thus increasing the danger of renewed inflationary pressures.   A gradual reduction of the Federal budget deficit, in line with present policy intentions, might enable a more expansionary monetary policy without endangering further progress in reducing inflation.   But easier credit conditions may not be sufficient.   Selective measures designed to reduce the risks attaching to investment may provide a stronger incentive to fixed capital formation.

While the demand outlook seems relatively satisfactory, prospects for reducing the underlying rate of inflation are less favourable.   Although the acceleration of prices in the first quarter was largely due to temporary influences and a reversal of certain dampening factors affecting the situation last year, there is a risk of revival of inflationary expectations.   Moreover, with unused capacity gradually being absorbed, marginal costs may rise and stronger price pressures develop.   These various risks underline the importance of close monitoring of price and wage developments as well as the implementation of an early warning system of emerging bottlenecks.

An important feature in the situation is that the underlying rate of inflation has remained about unchanged over the last two years.   New policy measures may therefore be required.   The announced anti-inflation programme could represent a useful adjunct to demand management. The proposed consultations between representatives of the authorities, labour and management may help to develop better understanding of the inflation problem and possible solutions. One way to break into the price/wage spiral might be to cut cost-related taxes. It would be essential, however, to ensure that cuts in taxes or fiscal charges are passed on to prices and that the resulting deceleration in inflation is reflected in subsequent wage claims.

Another major feature in the current economic situation is the change in the U.S. balance-of-payments position from a current account surplus of $11-12 billion in 1975 to an estimated deficit of around $14 billion in 1977. Apart from temporary influences, the swing in the current account can be ascribed to two main factors. First, there has been a change in the relative cyclical position of the U.S. economy. In line with the OECD medium-term strategy, the United States—with a strong overall external position and a rate of inflation below that of the average OECD country—has expanded rapidly over the last two years, thus aiding the world economic recovery and the international balance-of-payments adjustment process. From an international point of view, it is desirable that the United States, together with other better-placed countries, should continue to lead the world recovery, and that the U.S. current external account should remain in deficit for some time to come. The second factor behind the swing in the current account is the sharp rise in oil imports. Although related to the recovery of activity, this component reflects a structural weakness in the economy and is a matter of some concern. The Administration has therefore proposed an important programme of energy conservation and encouragement to domestic energy production. The rapid rise in oil imports underlines the need for early Congressional action on this matter.

Annex 1

CYCLICAL AND TREND MOVEMENTS IN PRODUCTIVITY

An important question about the recent deceleration of productivity growth in the United States is to what extent it is symptomatic of a fall in the "underlying" or long-run rate of productivity growth, and to what extent it is merely the result of the last recession.

To analyse this question, the Secretariat estimated an equation for productivity, distinguishing purely cyclical factors from the long-run trend of productivity. Since the fundamental determinants of the trend movement of productivity are difficult to identify, the trend was estimated simply by including a time variable[1]. The use of a linear time trend would, though, have been unduly restrictive, excluding the possibility of any change in the underlying movement of productivity. For this reason a quadratic time trend was used: this allows the underlying rate to change, albeit at a constant rate. Two variables were included to reflect the cyclical sensitivity of productivity. The first one was the gap between potential and actual GNP. Since some labour costs cannot be efficiently varied over a short range of output, higher rates of utilisation are likely to imply higher levels of productivity. Secondly, the costs connected with searching, hiring, training and lay-off affect the speed of adjusting employment to short-run changes in output, with the result that productivity is likely to be positively related to sharp short-run movements in output. To capture this effect, a ratio of output in the current quarter to a weighted average[2] of the previous four quarters was introduced. The equation estimated over the period 1952 Q1 to 1977 Q1 was:

(1) $$ln(X) = -0.59 - 0.56 ln(GAP) + 0.30 ln(DEV) + 0.0086T - 0.000019T^2$$
$$\quad\quad\quad\quad (17.34) \quad\quad (5.66) \quad\quad (47.38) \quad (15.05)$$

$R^2 = 0.9969$
$DW = 0.44$

where X is output per man hour in the private non-farm economy;

GAP is the ratio of potential GNP to actual GNP (1972 dollars);
DEV is $15Q/(8Q_{-1} + 4Q_{-2} + 2Q_{-3} + Q_{-4})$, Q denoting the index of output in the private non-farm economy;
T is a counting variable (1948 Q1=1, 1948 Q2=2 etc.) t-statistics are given in parenthesis; R^2 is corrected for degrees of freedom.

The negative sign of T^2 implies the existence of a steady decelerating trend in productivity from 2.8 per cent in the mid-1950s through 2.2 per cent in the mid-1960s to 1.7 per cent in the mid-1970s. However, the very low Durbin-Watson statistic indicates the presence of serial correlation and misspecification. Also the t-statistics are overstated so that the evidence for the existence of such a trend decline is somewhat weaker than the estimated equation and t-statistic of T^2 would suggest. A second problem is that T and T^2 are highly collinear, raising the possibilty that any bias in the coefficient of T would lead to an opposite bias in the coefficient of T^2. In particular, if the coefficient of T has an upward bias, the coefficient of T^2 will have a downward bias, thus exaggerating the trend decline in productivity[3]. As a check, therefore, on the robustness of the results, equation (1) was estimated in first difference form:

(2) $$ln\left[\frac{X_t}{X_{t-1}}\right] = 0.007 - 0.23 ln\left[\frac{GAP_t}{GAP_{t-1}}\right] + 0.33 ln\left[\frac{DEV_t}{DEV_{t-1}}\right] - 0.000023T$$
$$\quad\quad\quad\quad (5.06)\ (3.27) \quad\quad\quad\quad\quad (6.12) \quad\quad\quad\quad\quad (1.30)$$

$R^2 = 0.5970$
$DW = 1.58$

---

(1) It does not, of course, *explain* the factors underlying the trend of productivity.
(2) The weights were chosen so that successively distant quarters were given half as much weight as the quarter before: that is, the average was $(1/15) (8Q_{-1} + 4Q_{-2} + 2Q_{-3} + Q_{-4})$.
(3) That is the "true" coefficient of T^2 should be larger—in this case a smaller negative number.

This can be re-written in level form [comparable with equation (1)] as:

(2a) $$In(X) = -0.23In(GAP) + 0.33In(DEV) + 0.007T - 0.000012T^2 + C$$

Thus the evidence for a steady decelerating trend carries over, though it is somewhat weaker (the coefficient of T in equation (2) is negative and significant at the 10 per cent level in a onetail test). The deceleration is not, though, quite as sharp (the absolute value of the coefficient of T^2 is smaller in equation (2a) than in equation (1)). The deceleration revealed by equation (2) is from 2.4 per cent in the mid-1950s to 1.7 per cent in the mid-1970s. Both equations (1) and (2) do, though, put the underlying advance of productivity at 1.7 per cent today.

The cyclical sensitivity of productivity is also brought out by the equations. Both equations (1) and (2) indicate that a short-run change of output of one per cent[4] raises productivity by a third of a per cent. A reduction in the GNP gap of one per cent raises productivity by between a quarter and a half of a per cent.

Equation (1) was then used to decompose the observed movements of productivity in the last few years into their trend and cyclical components. The trend level of productivity was the level defined by equation (1) without the cyclical components:

$$In(X_{Trend}) = -0.59 + 0.0086T - 0.000019T^2$$

The cyclical component was then taken as the difference between this trend of productivity and the productivity estimated by equation (1) in full. This decomposition is shown in table 6 of the text.

Annex II

CHRONOLOGY OF MAIN ECONOMIC POLICY EVENTS

1976

January

The reserve requirement on time deposits with original maturities between 180 days and 4 years reduced from 3 to 2½ per cent.

Discount rate reduced from 6 to 5½ per cent.

In the State of the Union Message, the President called on Congress to cut taxes by a further $10 billion as from 1st July .in line with his last October proposals.

The Budget Message for fiscal year 1977 sent to Congress. Total Federal expenditures estimated to $394.2 billion a 5.5 per cent increase over FY 1976, and revenue expected to increase 18.1 per cent to $351.3 billion, reducing the budget deficit to $43 billion from an estimated $76 billion in FY 1976. (From FY 1977 on, fiscal year starts 1st October instead of 1st July as in the previous fiscal years).

February

The lower limit of the target range for M_1 reduced ½ percentage point for the year ending fourth quarter 1976.

April

Congress passed the first concurrent resolution on the fiscal year 1977 budget. The target ceiling for Federal outlays set at $413.6 billion with the recommended level of Federal revenues at $363.0 billion.

May

The upper limit of the target ranges for money growth lowered by ½ percentage point for M_1 and M_2. The growth ranges for the year ending in the first quarter of 1977 set at 4½ to 7 per cent for M_1, 7½ to 10 per cent for M_2 and 9 to 12 per cent for M_3.

July

The upper limits on the target ranges for M_2 and M_3 lowered by ½ and 1 percentage points respectively.

August

The Office of Management and the Budget (OMB) announced that the Federal deficit for FY 1976 fell $10.4 billion below last January's official projection to $65.6 billion. The discrepancy was attributed to lower-than-expected Federal spending.

October

The Tax Reform Act (1976) enacted: provisions included the permanent extension of last year's tax cuts and various other tax reforms.

Lower-than-expected Federal spending in the "transition quarter" (three months to 30th September) pushed the Federal government's deficit $3.4 billion below the level envisaged last January.

November

Mr. Jimmy Carter wins Presidential Election; large Democratic majority in both houses of the Congress.

The upper limit on target range for M_1 lowered by $\frac{1}{2}$ percentage point; those for M_2 and M_3 increased by the same amount.

The discount rate reduced to $5\frac{1}{4}$ per cent from $5\frac{1}{2}$ per cent.

1977

February

President Carter sent amended Federal budget to Congress. Spending planned to rise 14 per cent in FY 1977, and 10 per cent in FY 1978. With estimated receipts rising 16 per cent and 15 per cent respectively the proposed deficit to fall from $68.0 billion for FY 1977 to $57.7 billion for FY 1978. These changes reflected a proposed two-year $31.6 billion fiscal stimulus package: mainly tax reductions and rebates for FY 1977 and increased spending in FY 1978.

The lower limits for the target range of M_2 and M_3 lowered by $\frac{1}{2}$ percentage point.

April

In light of the withdrawal of the proposed $11.4 billion tax rebate and business tax credit, and of the continuing shortfalls in Federal expenditure, the OMB revised its projections for the Federal deficit: the deficit for FY 1977 reduced to $48.7 billion, but that for FY 1978 virtually unchanged at $57.9 billion.

An anti-inflation programme aimed at reducing the rate of inflation to 4-4½ per cent by the end of 1979 announced by the Administration. In addition to re-affirming his commitment to a balanced budget by FY 1981, the President outlined a number of specific measures to be taken by the Government while stressing the voluntary nature of the programme. The measures included:

(i)   government consultation with business and labour leaders to seek to lower inflation while supporting the rate of economic growth;
(ii)   enlarged role for the Council on Wage and Price Stability, to provide (through detailed industry studies) an early warning system for specific bottlenecks;
(iii) an examination of the possibility of commodity price stabilization, including legislation to allow strategic stockpiles (designed for wartime) to be used in the event of peacetime shortages;
(iv)   a review of the cost and efficiency effects of various government regulations.

Proposals for a comprehensive energy policy unveiled by the Administration. The twin objectives are:

(a)   to reduce the annual rate of growth of U.S. energy consumption from current levels of 4-5 per cent to 2 per cent by 1985, with petrol consumption to fall 10% from current levels;
(b)   encourage the development of alternative energy sources, aiming to reduce oil imports (averaging seven million barrels a day in 1976, and forecast to rise to between 12 and 15 million barrels by 1985 in the absence of further conservation measures) to 6 million barrels a day by 1985.

The detailed proposals are:

(i)   an increase in the price of domestic crude oil from the current price ceilings ($5.17 per barrel for "old" oil and about $11 per barrel for "new" oil) to world price levels (currently about $13.50 a barrel) by a gradually increasing wellhead tax;
(ii)   increase in the existing four-cents-a-gallon levy on petrol by up to five cents a year, to a maximum of 50 cents; increases triggered only if consumption exceeds annual target levels;
(iii) taxes on cars that are heavy fuel users, with rebates for more efficient vehicles;
(iv)   subsidies to encourage households' fuel economy and use of alternative energy sources, financed by the crude oil and petrol taxes; tax receipts remaining to be rebated on a per capita basis;
(v)   incentives for the development of alternative energy supplies;
(vi)   a stockpile of one billion barrels of oil to allow the U.S. to withstand "serious supply interruption" for 10 months.

May

The upper limits on the target range for M_2 and M_3 both reduced by $\frac{1}{2}$ percentage point.

The Administration announced plans for a major reform of social security financing, involving (over the next five years) higher taxes for employers and employees, with the heavier burden falling on the former.

President signs bill appropriating funds for the public spending part of the economic stimulus programme. Detailed appropriations, totalling $ 20.1 billion, included:

(*i*) $7.9 billion for public service jobs;
(*ii*) $4 billion for local public works;
(*iiiɟ*) $1.4 billion for employment and training programmes;
(*iv*) $4.9 billion for the Federal Government's regular programme of revenue sharing with states and local authorities;
(*vi*) $0.6 billion for special anti-recession revenue sharing.

Tax-cut bill enacted, reducing taxes by $2.6 billion in FY 1977 and $17.8 billion in FY 1978. Major provisions are:

(*i*) an increase in the standard deduction, retroactive to 1st January, and to be reflected in lower withholding rates from 1st June;
(*ii*) a tax credit for employers, up to $2 100 for each new worker hired in 1977 and 1978 after the number employed has grown 2 per cent from the previous year, with an annual maximum of $100 000 per firm;
(*iii*) extension through 1978 of the $35 per person general tax credit, the earned income credit for working poor with children and smaller tax rates for small corporations;
(*iv*) appropriations for an extra $2.25 billion special revenue sharing for states and localities with high unemployment.

STATISTICAL   ANNEX

Table A National Product and Expenditure in Current Prices

Billions of dollars; quarterly data seasonally adjusted at annual rates

	Personal consumption expenditures	Gross private domestic investment	New construction	Producers' durable equipment	Change in business inventories	Net exports of goods and services	Govt. purchases of goods and services	Federal	State and local	Gross national product
1960	324.9	76.4	43.2	29.5	3.8	4.4	100.3	53.7	46.5	506.0
1961	335.0	74.3	43.4	28.7	2.2	5.8	108.2	57.4	50.8	523.3
1962	355.2	85.2	46.9	31.8	6.5	5.4	118.0	63.7	54.3	563.8
1963	374.6	90.2	50.2	34.0	6.0	6.3	123.7	64.6	59.0	594.7
1964	400.4	96.6	52.6	38.2	5.8	8.9	129.8	65.2	64.6	635.7
1965	430.2	112.0	57.4	45.1	9.5	7.6	138.3	67.3	71.1	688.1
1966	464.8	124.5	58.0	52.2	14.3	5.1	158.7	78.8	79.8	753.0
1967	490.4	120.8	58.1	52.6	10.1	4.9	180.2	90.9	89.3	796.3
1968	535.9	131.5	66.1	57.7	7.7	2.3	198.7	98.0	100.7	868.5
1969	579.7	146.2	73.5	63.3	9.4	1.8	207.9	97.5	110.4	935.5
1970	618.8	140.8	74.2	62.8	3.8	3.9	218.9	95.6	123.2	982.4
1971	668.2	160.0	88.9	64.7	6.4	1.6	233.7	96.2	137.5	1 063.4
1972	733.0	188.3	104.5	74.3	9.4	-3.3	253.1	102.1	151.0	1 171.1
1973	809.9	220.0	115.1	87.0	17.9	7.1	269.5	102.2	167.3	1 306.6
1974	887.5	215.0	109.2	95.1	10.7	7.5	303.3	111.6	191.6	1 413.2
1975	973.2	183.7	103.2	95.1	-14.6	20.5	339.0	124.4	214.5	1 516.3
1976	1 079.7	239.6	123.0	104.7	11.9	6.6	365.6	133.4	232.2	1 691.6
1973: 1st quarter	787.2	210.6	114.3	84.5	11.8	1.7	265.8	104.2	161.6	1 265.3
2nd quarter	801.0	218.0	116.4	86.1	15.4	4.3	265.1	100.1	165.0	1 288.4
3rd quarter	818.2	220.0	116.5	88.1	15.4	10.0	269.3	100.1	169.3	1 317.5
4th quarter	833.1	231.5	113.3	89.1	29.0	12.7	277.8	104.4	173.5	1 355.1
1974: 1st quarter	853.3	216.4	111.1	92.7	12.6	15.0	288.0	106.1	181.9	1 372.7
2nd quarter	878.7	218.8	111.6	94.2	13.0	3.9	298.0	108.9	189.1	1 399.4
3rd quarter	906.8	213.3	109.1	96.8	7.3	2.9	308.6	113.5	195.1	1 431.6
4th quarter	911.1	211.5	105.0	96.7	9.7	8.1	318.5	118.1	200.4	1 449.2
1975: 1st quarter	933.2	172.4	99.7	94.9	-22.2	15.0	325.6	120.3	205.3	1 446.2
2nd quarter	960.3	164.4	99.8	94.6	-30.0	24.4	333.2	122.4	210.9	1 482.3
3rd quarter	987.3	196.7	104.4	94.3	-2.0	21.4	343.2	124.6	218.6	1 548.7
4th quarter	1 012.0	201.4	109.1	96.6	-4.3	21.0	353.8	130.4	223.4	1 588.2
1976: 1st quarter	1 043.6	229.6	114.5	100.2	14.8	8.4	354.7	129.2	225.5	1 636.2
2nd quarter	1 064.7	239.2	120.2	103.0	16.0	9.3	362.0	131.2	230.9	1 675.2
3rd quarter	1 088.5	247.0	124.9	107.0	15.1	4.7	369.6	134.5	235.0	1 709.8
4th quarter	1 122.0	242.8	132.5	108.6	1.7	4.2	376.2	138.9	237.4	1 745.1
1977: 1st quarter	1 159.1	267.9	136.8	117.4	13.8	-9.3	378.5	138.2	240.3	1 796.1

Source: US Department of Commerce Survey of Current Business.

Table B National Product and Expenditure in Constant Prices
Billions of 1972 dollars; quarterly data seasonally adjusted at annual rates

	Personal consumption expenditures	Gross private domestic investment	New construction	Producers' durable equipment	Change in business inventories	Net exports of goods and services	Govt. purchases of goods and services	Federal	State and local	Gross national product
1960	453.0	105.4	63.8	37.2	4.4	5.5	172.9	90.8	82.0	736.8
1961	462.2	103.6	64.4	36.3	2.9	6.7	182.8	95.6	87.1	755.3
1962	482.9	117.4	69.2	40.1	8.1	5.8	193.1	103.1	90.0	799.1
1963	501.4	124.5	74.0	42.7	7.8	7.3	197.6	102.2	95.4	830.7
1964	528.7	132.1	77.1	47.7	7.3	10.9	202.7	100.6	102.1	874.4
1965	558.1	150.1	82.8	56.0	11.3	8.2	209.6	100.5	109.1	925.9
1966	586.1	161.3	81.0	63.6	16.7	4.3	229.3	112.5	116.8	981.0
1967	603.2	152.7	78.3	62.4	12.0	3.5	248.3	125.3	123.1	1 007.7
1968	633.4	159.5	84.8	66.1	8.7	−0.4	259.2	128.3	130.9	1 051.8
1969	655.4	168.0	87.2	70.3	10.6	−1.3	256.7	121.8	134.9	1 078.8
1970	668.9	154.7	83.2	67.2	4.3	1.4	250.2	110.7	139.5	1 075.3
1971	691.9	166.8	93.9	66.3	6.6	−0.6	249.4	103.9	145.5	1 107.5
1972	733.0	188.3	104.5	74.3	9.4	−3.3	253.1	102.1	151.0	1 171.1
1973	767.7	207.2	105.2	85.5	16.5	7.6	252.5	96.6	155.5	1 235.0
1974	759.1	182.0	87.1	86.5	8.5	16.5	256.4	95.3	161.1	1 214.0
1975	770.3	137.8	75.1	74.7	−12.0	22.6	261.0	95.7	165.2	1 191.7
1976	813.7	170.9	85.2	77.7	8.1	16.0	264.1	96.7	167.4	1 264.7
1973: 1st quarter	767.7	204.6	108.7	84.2	11.7	2.3	255.2	100.7	154.5	1 229.8
2nd quarter	766.8	207.4	107.5	85.1	14.8	5.7	251.2	96.3	154.9	1 231.1
3rd quarter	770.4	204.9	104.6	86.2	14.1	9.3	251.8	95.2	156.6	1 236.3
4th quarter	765.9	211.8	99.7	86.7	25.4	12.9	252.0	94.3	157.7	1 242.6
1974: 1st quarter	761.8	194.8	94.5	88.9	11.4	18.4	255.4	95.3	160.1	1 230.4
2nd quarter	761.9	187.9	90.5	88.1	9.4	14.9	256.1	94.7	161.4	1 220.8
3rd quarter	764.7	176.2	84.2	86.9	5.1	14.9	257.1	95.8	161.3	1 212.9
4th quarter	748.1	169.1	79.1	82.0	8.0	17.7	256.9	95.4	161.5	1 191.7
1975: 1st quarter	754.6	129.3	72.9	76.9	−20.5	20.1	257.1	94.8	162.2	1 161.1
2nd quarter	767.5	126.2	72.9	74.5	−21.2	24.3	259.1	95.3	163.8	1 177.1
3rd quarter	775.3	148.7	76.2	73.5	−1.0	22.8	262.4	95.6	166.9	1 209.3
4th quarter	783.9	147.0	78.6	73.8	−5.5	23.1	265.2	97.2	168.0	1 219.2
1976: 1st quarter	800.7	167.1	81.2	75.5	10.4	16.6	261.9	95.4	166.6	1 246.3
2nd quarter	808.6	171.7	83.6	77.0	11.1	16.0	263.6	96.0	167.7	1 260.0
3rd quarter	815.7	175.2	85.8	79.2	10.2	15.7	265.5	97.3	168.2	1 272.2
4th quarter	829.7	169.8	90.0	79.0	0.9	15.5	265.3	98.1	167.3	1 280.4
1977: 1st quarter	843.8	183.1	89.4	84.5	9.2	10.9	262.4	96.4	166.0	1 300.3

Source: US Department of Commerce *Survey of Current Business.*

Table C   **Monetary Indicators**

Seasonally adjusted (in billions of dollars)

| | Money supply[1] | | | Gross Loans and Investments at Commercial Banks[2] [8] | | | |
| | | | | | | Securities | |
	Total	Currency	Demand deposits	Total[3]	Loans[3] [4]	US Treasury	Other[4]
1969: December[5]	208.6	46.1	162.5	401.7	279.1	51.5	71.1
1970: December	219.6	49.1	170.5	435.5	291.7	57.9	85.9
1971: December	233.8	52.6	181.3	485.7	320.9	60.6	104.2
1972: December	255.3	56.9	198.4	558.0	378.9	62.6	116.5
1973: December	270.5	61.5	209.0	633.4	449.0	54.5	129.9
1974: December[6] [7]	283.1	67.8	215.3	690.4	500.2	50.4	139.8
1975: December	294.8	73.7	221.0	721.1	496.9	79.4	144.8
1976: January	295.1	74.2	220.9	723.3	497.3	81.0	145.0
February	296.6	75.0	221.6	726.7	497.8	84.4	144.5
March	298.1	75.7	222.4	731.2	499.7	88.2	143.3
April	301.8	76.7	225.2	734.5	500.5	90.0	144.0
May	303.5	77.3	226.2	737.6	500.6	93.0	144.0
June	303.2	77.6	225.6	738.8	500.7	94.0	144.1
July	305.0	78.1	226.8	743.1	504.7	92.7	145.7
August	306.3	78.6	227.7	748.7	507.6	95.0	146.1
September	306.9	79.2	227.7	759.8	517.9	94.4	147.5
October	310.5	79.8	230.7	767.6	525.8	93.8	148.0
November	310.6	80.3	230.3	778.8	533.1	95.4	150.3
December	312.8	80.6	232.1	784.4	538.9	97.3	148.2
1977: January	314.3	81.3	233.0	786.6p	540.9p	96.9p	148.8p
February	314.5	82.0	232.5	796.4p	545.4p	101.5p	149.5p
March	316.1	82.4	233.7	803.0p	551.0p	103.6p	148.4p
April	321.3	83.3	238.1	812.4p	557.7p	102.8p	151.9p
May				819.4p	562.1p	104.6p	152.7p

1   Average of daily figures.
2   Data are for last Wednesday of month.
3   Adjusted to exclude domestic commercial interbank loans.
4   Beginning June, 1969, data for loans and investments at commercial banks revised to include all bank premises subsidiaries and other significant majority owned subsidiaries; earlier data include commercial banks only. Series also changed to include gross loans and investments without the deduction of valuation reserves rather than net of valuation reserves as done previously.
5   Beginning June 30, 1971, Farmers Home Administration insured notes totalling approximately $700 million are included in "Other securities" rather than in "Loans".
6   Data beginning June 30, 1974, include one large mutual savings bank that merged with a nonmember commercial bank. As of that date there were increases of about $500 million in loans, $100 million in "Other securities", and $600 million in "Total loans and investments".
7   As of Oct. 31, 1974, "Total loans and investments", of all commercial banks were reduced by $1.5 billion in connection with the liquidation of one large bank. Reductions in other items were: "Total loans" $1.0 billion (of which $0.5 billion was in "Commercial and industrial loans"), and "Other securities" $0.5 billion. In late November "Commercial and industrial loans" were increased by $0.1 billion as a result of loan reclassifications at another large bank.
8   The Federal Reserve has revised data beginning January 1976 but has published figures only for September 1976-May 1977.

Source: Board of Governors of the Federal Reserve System *Federal Reserve Bulletin.*

Table D   Balance of Payments, OECD Basis

Millions of dollars

	1967	1968	1969	1970	1971	1972	1973	1974	1975	1976
Exports, fob	30 666	33 626	36 414	42 469	43 319	49 381	71 410	98 310	107 088	114 692
Imports, fob	26 866	32 991	35 807	39 866	45 579	55 797	70 499	103 679	98 058	123 916
Trade balance	3 800	635	607	2 603	-2 260	-6 416	911	-5 369	9 030	-9 224
Services, net[1][2]	540	1 008	370	335	2 004	462	2 993	8 939	7 287	13 626
Balance on goods and services	4 340	1 643	977	2 938	-256	-5 954	3 904	3 570	16 317	4 401
Private transfers, net	-879	-836	-939	-1 096	-1 117	-1 103	-1 252	-1 016	-913	-943
Official transfers, net[2]	-2 246	-2 115	-2 055	-2 198	-2 585	-2 745	-2 631	-3 413	-3 707	-4 062
Current balance	1 215	-1 308	-2 017	-356	-3 957	-9 802	22	-859	11 697	-604
Long-term capital (excl. spec. trans.)	-4 938	-1 161	-1 973	-3 640	-7 026	-1 424	-1 741	-8 992	-7 772	-9 482
(a) Private[3]	-2 712	-1 207	-447	-1 677	-4 444	-247	-12	-7 180	-6 679	-12 013
(b) Official[2][4]	-2 226	-2 368	-1 526	-1 963	-2 582	-1 177	-1 729	-1 812	-1 093	-2 531
Basic balance	-3 723	-2 469	-3 990	-3 996	-10 983	-11 226	-1 719	-9 851	3 925	-10 086
Non-monetary short-term private capital	1	-223	389	892	-1 076	-590	-1 245	-920	-1 255	-1 329
Non-monetary short-term official capital										
Errors and omissions	-128	507	-1 430	-402	-9 609	-1 790	-2 107	4 557	4 570	10 495
Balance on non-monetary transactions	-3 850	-2 185	-5 031	-3 506	-21 668	-13 606	-5 071	-6 214	7 240	-920
Private monetary institutions short-term capital	877	3 694	7 859	-7 443	-9 029	2 406	-5 072	-2 303	-10 167	-7 842
(a) Assets[5]	-730	-105	-867	-1 122	-2 368	-2 199	-5 047	-18 311	-11 114	-18 644
(b) Liabilities[5]	1 607	3 799	8 726	-6 321	-6 661	4 605	4 475	16 008	947	10 802
Balance on official settlements	-2 973	1 509	2 828	-10 949	-30 697	-11 200	-5 643	-8 517	-2 927	-8 762
Total liabilities to foreign national official agencies[6]	3 345	-758	-1 541	7 815	27 427	10 866	5 145	9 953	3 534	—
Use of IMF credit[7]	22	-3	-11	-453	-22	-544	—	—	—	—
Special transactions[8]	-447	132	-87	244	227	137	289	1	—	—
Miscellaneous official accounts	—	—	—	—	—	—	—	—	—	11 292
Allocation of SDRs	—	—	—	867	717	710	—	—	—	—
Change in reserves (+ = increase)	-52	880	1 187	-2 477	-2 348	-547	-209	1 434	607	2 530
(a) Gold	-1 170	-1 173	967	-787	-866	-547	—	—	—	—
(b) Currency assets	1 024	1 183	-814	-2 152	-381	-35	-233	-3	75	240
(c) Reserve positions in IMF	94	870	1 034	-389	-1 350	-153	33	1 265	466	2 212
(d) Special Drawing Rights	—	—	—	851	249	703	-9	172	66	78

1 Includes debt obligations payable by the United Kingdom but waived ($66 million in 1968) but excludes reinvested earnings.
2 Excluding transactions related to cancellation of Indian debt in 1974 Q1: investment income: 17 million official transfers:—2 010 million long-term off, capital: 1 992 million in 1974 Q2: excluding other extraordinary grants estimated at: off transfers:—746 million official long-term capital: 746 million.
3 Includes changes in foreign long-term claims on US commercial banks. Excludes liquication of UK govt. portfolio ($463 million in 1969).
4 Includes changes in investment by international organisations in US government agency bonds, includes debt obligations payable by the UK but waived ($72 million in 1968).
5 Excludes liabilities to foreign national official agencies. Includes liquid liabilities of other sectors than banking sector to foreign non-official institutions and persons (including liquid liabilities to non-monetary international and regional organisations).
6 Includes liabilities to BIS.
7 Includes gold deposits and investment by the IMF.
8 *Special transactions:* 1967: Debt prepayments: $6 million liquication of UK Government portfolio: $-453 million; 1968: Debt prepayments: $269 million UK waiver: $-137 million; 1969: Debt prepayments: $-87 million; 1970: Debt prepayments: $244 million; 1971: Debt prepayments: $226 million; 1972: Debt prepayments: $137 million; 1973: Debt prepayments: $289 million.
NOTE Very recent revisions to balance of payments statistics included in the shorter text table (4) have not been carried through in this table.
Sources: US Department of Commerce *Survey of Current Business*; Federal Reserve System, *Federal Reserve Bulletin*.

INTERNATIONAL COMPARISONS

OECD SALES AGENTS
DÉPOSITAIRES DES PUBLICATIONS DE L'OCDE

ARGENTINA – ARGENTINE
Carlos Hirsch S.R.L., Florida 165,
BUENOS-AIRES. ☎33-1787-2391 Y 30-7122
AUSTRALIA – AUSTRALIE
International B.C.N. Library Suppliers Pty Ltd.,
161 Sturt St., South MELBOURNE, Vic. 3205. ☎699-6388
658 Pittwater Road, BROOKVALE NSW 2100. ☎ 938 2267
AUSTRIA – AUTRICHE
Gerold and Co., Graben 31, WIEN 1. ☎52.22.35
BELGIUM – BELGIQUE
Librairie des Sciences,
Coudenberg 76-78, B 1000 BRUXELLES 1. ☎512-05-60
BRAZIL – BRÉSIL
Mestre Jou S.A., Rua Guaipá 518,
Caixa Postal 24090, 05089 SAO PAULO 10. ☎ 261-1920
Rua Senador Dantas 19 s/205-6, RIO DE JANEIRO GB.
☎ 232-07. 32
CANADA
Renouf Publishing Company Limited,
2182 St. Catherine Street West,
MONTREAL, Quebec H3H 1M7 ☎(514) 937-3519
DENMARK – DANEMARK
Munksgaards Boghandel,
Nørregade 6, 1165 KØBENHAVN K. ☎(01) 12 69 70
FINLAND – FINLANDE
Akateeminen Kirjakauppa
Keskuskatu 1, 00100 HELSINKI 10. ☎625.901
FRANCE
Bureau des Publications de l'OCDE,
2 rue André-Pascal, 75775 PARIS CEDEX 16.
☎524.81.67
Principal correspondant :
13602 AIX-EN-PROVENCE : Librairie de l'Université.
☎26.18.08
GERMANY – ALLEMAGNE
Verlag Weltarchiv G.m.b.H.
D 2000 HAMBURG 36, Neuer Jungfernstieg 21.
☎ 040-35-62-500
GREECE – GRÈCE
Librairie Kauffmann, 28 rue du Stade,
ATHÈNES 132. ☎322.21.60
HONG-KONG
Government Information Services,
Sales and Publications Office, Beaconsfield House, 1st floor,
Queen's Road, Central. ☎H-233191
ICELAND – ISLANDE
Snaebjörn Jónsson and Co., h.f.,
Hafnarstraeti 4 and 9, P.O.B. 1131, REYKJAVIC.
☎13133/14281/11936
INDIA – INDE
Oxford Book and Stationery Co.:
NEW DELHI, Scindia House. ☎45896
CALCUTTA, 17 Park Street. ☎240832
IRELAND - IRLANDE
Eason and Son, 40 Lower O'Connell Street,
P.O.B. 42. DUBLIN 1. ☎74 39 35
ISRAËL
Emanuel Brown: 35 Allenby Road, TEL AVIV. ☎51049/54082
also at:
9. Shlomzion Hamalka Street, JERUSALEM. ☎234807
48 Nahlath Benjamin Street, TEL AVIV. ☎53276
ITALY – ITALIE
Libreria Commissionaria Sansoni:
Via Lamarmora 45, 50121 FIRENZE. ☎579751
Via Bartolini 29, 20155 MILANO. ☎365083
Sous-dépositaires :
Editrice e Libreria Herder,
Piazza Montecitorio 120, 00 186 ROMA. ☎674628
Libreria Hoepli, Via Hoepli 5, 20121 MILANO. ☎365446
Libreria Lattes, Via Garibaldi 3, 10122 TORINO. ☎519274
La diffusione delle edizioni OCDE è inoltre assicurata dalle migliori
librerie nelle città più importanti.

JAPAN – JAPON
OECD Publications Centre,
Akasaka Park Building, 2-3-4 Akasaka, Minato-ku,
TOKYO 107. ☎586-2016
KOREA - CORÉE
Pan Korea Book Corporation,
P.O.Box n°101 Kwangwhamun, SÉOUL. ☎72-7369
LEBANON – LIBAN
Documenta Scientifica/Redico,
Edison Building. Bliss Street, P.O.Box 5641, BEIRUT.
☎354429–344425
THE NETHERLANDS – PAYS-BAS
W.P. Van Stockum,
Buitenhof 36, DEN HAAG. ☎070-65.68.08
NEW ZEALAND - NOUVELLE-ZÉLANDE
The Publications Manager,
Government Printing Office,
WELLINGTON: Mulgrave Street (Private Bag),
World Trade Centre, Cubacade, Cuba Street,
Rutherford House, Lambton Quay, ☎737-320
AUCKLAND: Rutland Street (P.O.Box 5344), ☎32.919
CHRISTCHURCH: 130 Oxford Tce (Private Bag), ☎50.331
HAMILTON: Barton Street (P.O.Box 857), ☎80.103
DUNEDIN: T & G Building, Princes Street (P.O.Box 1104),
☎78.294
NORWAY – NORVÈGE
Johan Grundt Tanums Bokhandel,
Karl Johansgate 41/43, OSLO 1. ☎02-332980
PAKISTAN
Mirza Book Agency, 65 Shahrah Quaid-E-Azam, LAHORE 3.
☎66839
PHILIPPINES
R.M. Garcia Publishing House, 903 Quezon Blvd. Ext.,
QUEZON CITY, P.O.Box 1860 – MANILA. ☎99.98.47
PORTUGAL
Livraria Portugal, Rua do Carmo 70-74, LISBOA 2. ☎360582/3
SPAIN – ESPAGNE
Mundi-Prensa Libros, S.A.
Castelló 37, Apartado 1223, MADRID-1. ☎275.46.55
Libreria Bastinos, Pelayo, 52, BARCELONA 1. ☎222.06.00
SWEDEN – SUÈDE
AB CE FRITZES KUNGL HOVBOKHANDEL,
Box 16 356, S 103 27 STH, Regeringsgatan 12,
DS STOCKHOLM. ☎08/23 89 00
SWITZERLAND – SUISSE
Librairie Payot, 6 rue Grenus, 1211 GENÈVE 11. ☎022-31.89.50
TAIWAN – FORMOSE
National Book Company,
84-5 Sing Sung Rd., Sec. 3, TAIPEI 107. ☎321.0698
TURKEY – TURQUIE
Librairie Hachette,
469 Istiklal Caddesi, Beyoglu, ISTANBUL. ☎44.94.70
et 14 E Ziya Gökalp Caddesi, ANKARA. ☎12.10.80
UNITED KINGDOM – ROYAUME-UNI
H.M. Stationery Office, P.O.B. 569,
LONDON SE1 9 NH. ☎01-928-6977, Ext.410
or
49 High Holborn, LONDON WC1V 6 HB (personal callers)
Branches at: EDINBURGH, BIRMINGHAM, BRISTOL,
MANCHESTER, CARDIFF, BELFAST.
UNITED STATES OF AMERICA
OECD Publications Center, Suite 1207, 1750 Pennsylvania Ave.,
N.W. WASHINGTON, D.C.20006. ☎(202)298-8755
VENEZUELA
Libreria del Este, Avda. F. Miranda 52, Edificio Galipán,
CARACAS 106. ☎32 23 01/33 26 04/33 24 73
YUGOSLAVIA – YOUGOSLAVIE
Jugoslovenska Knjiga, Terazije 27, P.O.B. 36, BEOGRAD.
☎621-992

Les commandes provenant de pays où l'OCDE n'a pas encore désigné de dépositaire peuvent être adressées à :
OCDE, Bureau des Publications, 2 rue André-Pascal, 75775 PARIS CEDEX 16.
Orders and inquiries from countries where sales agents have not yet been appointed may be sent to:
OECD, Publications Office, 2 rue André-Pascal, 75775 PARIS CEDEX 16.

DOCUMENTS OFFICIELS

 1979

GOVERNMENT
PUBLICATIONS

OECD   PUBLICATIONS
2, rue André-Pascal
75775 PARIS CEDEX 16
No. 39,195   1977.

●

PRINTED IN FRANCE